The
Pretty
Victory

RODALE
NEW YORK

# The *Pretty* Victory

## 100-Day Guide
*to* Recenter Yourself
and Find Your Purpose

# Pretty Vee

Published in the United States by Rodale Books, an imprint of Random House, a division of Penguin Random House LLC, New York.

Rodale & Plant with colophon is a registered trademark of Penguin Random House LLC.

LIBRARY OF CONGRESS CATALOGING-IN-PUBLICATION DATA
Names: Pretty Vee, author.
Title: The pretty victory / Pretty Vee.
Description: First edition. | New York, NY: Rodale, [2025] |
Identifiers: LCCN 2024035573 (print) | LCCN 2024035574
(ebook) | ISBN 9780593798089 (hardcover) |
ISBN 9780593798096 (ebook)
Subjects: LCSH: Self-realization. | Self-realization—Religious
aspects. | Spiritual life.
Classification: LCC BF637.S4 P745 2025 (print) | LCC BF637.S4
(ebook) | DDC 242/.2—dc23/eng/20240903
LC record available at https://lccn.loc.gov/2024035573
LC ebook record available at https://lccn.loc.gov/2024035574

Printed in the United States of America on acid-free paper

RodaleBooks.com | RandomHouseBooks.com

1st Printing

First Edition

*Book design by Susan Turner*

The
Pretty
Victory

# INTRODUCTION

## Finding Your Way to Pretty Victory

I believe that everything is a message. I can look up at a cloud moving across the sky and know it's telling me that change is coming. I can get a phone call from a friend I haven't heard from in a long time, and I'll know she's got something to tell me that'll set me on my path— and she probably doesn't even know it. I can pass a stranger on the street and exchange a smile, and something about that moment will change both of us for the better, because even just a little bit of kindness makes a difference.

So that's how I know this: When you picked up this book, you got a sign. Now you just need to know how to read it. Whether somebody gave it to you as a present or you saw it at the store—that was a message: for you to stop delaying, stop feeling like you don't have a voice in your own life. It's time for you to find your purpose.

Listen, we all get lost along the way. We all need healing.

In our journeys through life, we all accumulate wounds and scars. But over the course of these hundred days, you're going to follow the path back to your own center. You're going to heal what's been hurt inside you—and that will help you grow into what you were always meant to be.

> You are meant to be set free.
> You are meant to be healed.
> You are meant to be whole.
> You are meant to be on your path.
> You are meant to let your voice resonate, loud and clear, for all to hear.
> You are meant to attain your own *Pretty Victory*.

## What's a Pretty Victory?

I can hear you asking, "All right, Vee—what is that, anyway?" I'm going to break it down for you.

Hearing the word *pretty* makes a lot of people think of something soft or sweet. Something that's all about how you *look*, like "Oh, isn't she so pretty?" And there's nothing wrong with wanting to look good or feel good. When I first started to make it in the entertainment industry, I needed a way to stand out, something that would help build my brand. By choosing to go by Pretty Vee, I wasn't rejecting the idea of being pretty in that way—I was embracing it.

But that's not *all* it was either. For me, pretty doesn't

have anything to do with makeup or cute clothes. It's not about the glam. It's about who someone is, the light that shines out from inside. It is about embodying an inner radiance.

Pretty isn't about the superficial. It's about fearlessness, audacity, and the celebration of your unique beauty. It's about being outstanding, marvelous, powerful. A friend, a sister. A cousin, a listener, and a believer in Jesus Christ.

It's a reminder that within each of us, there is a source of beauty that extends far beyond physical appearance.

Pretty Vee is someone fearless, bold, and beautiful. She's outstanding, marvelous, powerful, unique. She's a friend, a sister. A cousin, a listener, and a believer in Jesus Christ.

To have a Pretty Vee in your life means to have someone you can count on, someone who is unwavering in their support and who unapologetically embraces their true self. That's what all my people are to me—that's what *you* are to me: pretty, inside and out.

Pretty means someone who loves and is loved, who is always there, and who is absolutely, unforgettably, perfectly *herself*.

*Pretty is you.*

And how do you get to victory? Well, that's about stepping *up*.

Success doesn't come from luck. Being victorious requires doing the work. You've got to earn it. It calls for effort, determination, and resilience. It's about embracing challenges and personal growth, ascending the ladder of knowledge while holding true to your values and beliefs.

You've got to have the strength as well as the voice to speak for the voiceless—even if once upon a time "the voiceless" meant you. You are victorious when you have room to grow.

You are brave. You are a conqueror.

A Pretty Victory isn't always a rosy, glamorous, easy ride. It involves grappling with pain. It involves ugly things. It requires going through a journey of rejection and self-discovery. But once you start discovering who you are through the not-so-good times, even that journey through ugliness will become pretty—because it's ultimately guiding you toward triumph.

That's where you're going. That's where these hundred days will take you. Embrace it all—the ups and downs, the beauty and the struggle—and let this exploration lead you to the person you were always meant to be. In the end, we will celebrate the victory that will be undeniably, beautifully yours.

## How to Use This Book

We're going to be together for one hundred days. Right now, I bet that seems like a really long time, but I promise you, it will go by in a blink. I thought about how long this journey should be—thirty days of devotionals? A full year?—and I settled on one hundred days because that's how long it took me to start really developing some new habits, new ways of thinking, and new confidence in myself and my abilities. After one hundred days, you'll see the change in your life.

Each one of these hundred days will offer you something to think on and something to lift you up. You'll find words of encouragement and calls to action that propel you up off the couch so you start putting in the hard work to make your dreams come true. There may also be some hard truths here that force you to recognize what's been holding you back.

You'll also have space to journal, to write out what the experience makes you feel and what you're going to do about that. Are there specific steps for you to take that very day? Are you going to put something in your calendar? Are you going to call a friend, go out on a run, cross that item off your list, make that difficult phone call, write that email, work that connection?

And each day will end with a Pretty Prayer. It might be something you copy onto a Post-it note and stick to your mirror or carry around with you in your pocket for the day, so it can see you through whatever comes at you.

Within the hundred days, you'll also find words of wisdom from some of my victorious friends, like Charlamagne Tha God, Issa Rae, and Dwyane Wade. They'll be dropping some gems along the way, sharing what makes them victorious, and I hope their insights will infuse you with hope and sustain your inspiration.

You don't need to wait until New Year's to start. You're gonna start right now. Today.

But you've got to go through these hundred days step by step. They are laid out in a very specific order, and they are going to require you to buckle down. Pick your hundred days and *stick to them*. On Day One, you do Day One. On Day Two, you tackle Day Two—not on Day Three or Week Three. You gotta do this *every day*. That's the only way you're going to forever change the way you think— about yourself, your life, your purpose, and how you're going to share your gifts with the world. If you get waylaid, that's okay; life's gonna be lifin' (I get it). But then you pick this book up and you keep going. Over the course of these hundred days, you're going to build up the strength to get through the delays and the struggles. You're going to build up your faith so it can keep propelling you forward even when you feel like you've run into a brick wall. (Hint: Sometimes you gotta go around.)

## Where I Come From

I call myself Pretty Vee—I *am* Pretty Vee—but I was born Davana Excell. (I know you're probably wondering where "Davana" comes from, but we'll get to that in the next book.) My roots trace back to the bustling city of Miami, where I was raised by Caribbean parents. My upbringing was characterized by strong values and a sense of discipline. My mother, in particular, was a firm presence in my life, and my father was equally stern—they taught me the importance of accepting personal responsibility and taking care of myself.

As the youngest child in the family, I was often caught up in my own world, lost in thought even at the tender age of seven. I found myself sitting alone, pondering the questions of existence, trying to understand the world: Why are we here? What is our purpose? What is *my* purpose? I was filled with curiosity. In the midst of my inner exploration, I found solace and guidance in faith, as my mom is a pastor. Religion became my path toward understanding the world and finding answers to my many questions. I always felt the presence of Jesus, guiding me on a path toward self-discovery and purpose.

I was outspoken and confident. Even when I was alone, I imagined I was surrounded by other people. I would picture myself onstage, talking to a crowd, giving interviews—that dreamer in me was always there, always imagining something big and dazzling. It would get me in trouble sometimes, as my daydreaming tendencies led to moments of inattentiveness in the classroom. And then, as I got older and realized I could make people laugh with the things I made up in my head, I got in even more trouble, clowning around in the middle of class.

That was such a wonderful feeling, though—making somebody laugh or, better yet, making a whole *room* laugh. It was exhilarating, and I could feel that it was what I was supposed to do. Even when my name was being yelled and

I was getting in trouble, I was okay with that, because I knew it meant there was something special about me. I had something in me that made other people want to turn around and look, to see what I would come up with next.

My self-assurance was strengthened by my mother's unwavering belief in me. She recognized the gift Jesus had bestowed on me and took every opportunity to nurture it. My mother is such an anointed believer; anyone who has been my friend—young and old—knows about her faith. She enrolled me in recitals, ballet classes, and music lessons, doing everything she could to help grow my creativity.

I was blessed with loving parents. They both wanted what was best for me, but they had very different visions for what that might be. My father is a very practical man and was always looking out for my safety first—did I have what I needed? Did I have a roof over my head and food to eat? When it came to my future, he thought in the same practical, realistic terms: Would I be able to make money? He didn't want me to have to depend on anyone or anything. It wasn't that he didn't believe in me—he just wanted me to play it safe and to have stability and financial security. He said, "You're funny, but you being funny ain't gonna make no money."

But once I started turning funny into money, he got it. He saw me on a Times Square billboard in New York City, and he said, "Now this girl is making a living for herself."

When I was just a little kid with these big, unrealistic dreams, though, it was hard for him to see that, and he

just wanted me to be able to make a good living for myself. He wanted me to hit the books and study hard, and I appreciated that (even if I still got into trouble at school sometimes).

Not everyone in my life had such good intentions. There were people who would put me down. They undermined me, trying to shatter my dreams with their harsh words. One particular incident in high school comes to mind, as an altercation led someone to tell me, cruelly, that I would "never amount to anything."

That day, I sat there and thought about what he said. I was so young, and back then I felt like I had to prove myself, to validate my worth. I *wasn't* a success yet, and I felt like I had to transform my dreams into reality before I was worth anything. I wasn't living as if it were *already* true. I wanted to be accepted, to feel whole . . . So if someone said something good and kind to me, I latched on to that. And if they said something hurtful to me, I latched on to that too. I didn't have the belief in myself that I have now. I needed to make a home for that belief, give it an address inside myself. But as I said, I was young.

People's voices have an impact, particularly when you're feeling voiceless.

My mom came and found me that day. She sat beside me, took my hand, and gave me her voice and her unwavering belief in me at a time when I didn't have my own. She gave me the strength to stand up and turn that negative moment into something positive.

I didn't allow the negative voices or hurtful comments to hold me back; instead, I used them as catalysts for growth and determination. I went to college and earned my degree while hosting my own radio show—and that's where I began to hear and amplify my own voice.

## Tapping into My Mind and Meeting Angels

I'd always envisioned myself as harboring a creative entity within, a little being residing in the attic of my mind, crafting intricate stories and inventing the vibrant characters I play today. When I was young, this creative spirit was a source of fear, a peculiar presence that set me apart from the other kids. Everyone around me seemed so sure of everything, and nobody else created stories and characters in their minds the way I did. Why did I do this? What was real, and what was made up? I didn't understand it.

But by the time I got to college, I'd learned to embrace my own creativity. I understood that it was a God-given gift, a spring of potential waiting to be harnessed and honed. I began to tap into it, recognizing it as an integral part of who I am. At Saint Augustine's University in Raleigh, North Carolina, I became an active part of the campus community. I hosted my own radio show, a platform that allowed me to share my voice and humor with the world. My voice became a part of the soundtrack of the college, infusing laughter and joy into the lives of those who tuned in, bringing everyone together. I felt an indescribable sense

of fulfillment, and I was beginning to live in alignment with my true purpose.

Within the campus community, one individual stood out as an angel among us: a man by the name of Mr. Daniels. He was the janitor at Saint Augustine's, but beyond that job, he possessed a heart of boundless compassion and infectious vitality that touched everyone he encountered. Mr. Daniels was a constant figure on Saint Augustine's campus, engaging in conversations with students and offering a listening ear, and on fried chicken Thursdays, he would often ask, "Can I pray with you?" He'd speak with us and laugh with us, and he would sow into us. He had a mighty gift from God, and he spoke into so many lives.

My mom was prophetically inclined. She told me I was going to be in the arts, and Mr. Daniels confirmed that. He told me that the world would love me and that I would spread joy into countless hearts and minds. He confirmed what my mom had said and told me that I would be a force to be reckoned with, and his words ignited a fire within me.

I remember one day, he came up to me and offered me fifty dollars. I said, "Mr. Daniels, I can't accept this." In his wisdom, he simply replied, "God told me you haven't been eating." My stomach growled in agreement, and in that moment, I realized the depth of his insight and compassion. I accepted his gift with gratitude, understanding that it was a divine act of kindness, a manifestation of God's care.

Mr. Daniels didn't know anything about me or what

was going on in my life. I hadn't talked to him about my financial troubles. He just knew—because God spoke to him. And that taught me something about accepting help—because if Jesus thought I mattered enough to put the thought into someone's mind, then I must be worth something. I should take that helping hand being offered.

Our connection endured even after my college years, and to this day, Mr. Daniels and I are still in touch. He entrusted me with his phone number, which was no small thing to me back when I was just some kid he knew. After I graduated from college—with a vision but no set plan for my next step—I reached out to him for guidance. Mr. Daniels gave me the best advice: he told me to read the Bible, to center myself, to get myself to a place where I could hear Jesus Christ and heal the voices of negativity.

He follows me on Instagram now, and I always tell him, "Mr. Daniels, you do *not* want to see my page—it is not angel friendly." He doesn't care. He just wants to check in with me from time to time as he goes about his own life, doing his ministry work. His enduring support and spiritual guidance continue to hold a special place in my heart, and our conversations remain a source of inspiration and strength. In the tapestry of my life, Mr. Daniels is a thread of divine kindness and wisdom, a reminder that even in the most unexpected places, we can find angels among us, guiding us toward our true purpose.

# A Delay Is Not a Denial

When I graduated from college, I felt as though the world had laid out a red carpet just for me. I had a crystal-clear vision of my future: I was destined to have my own radio show, and I was going to be famous and transform the lives of everyone who tuned in to hear my voice. This vision was not just a dream; it was a conviction. I *knew* with unwavering certainty that this was how my life was meant to unfold, and with that knowledge came the expectation that it would happen effortlessly.

It didn't. I knew what my gift was, and I had faith in it . . . but I didn't know how to use it. I didn't have a platform to showcase my talents, which meant that I could be as funny and as entertaining as I wanted, but nobody was there to hear me.

That sudden silence hit me like a punch to the chest. During my time in college, I had been a whirlwind of activity, in the center of everything, and once I got out and real life began, the contrast was tough. It was so quiet. I felt like I was nothing. My mind, which had been so lively and creative, now cycled through poisonous thoughts that tormented me through sleepless nights that stretched into months.

I thought I would get a job so easily, and when that didn't happen, it felt like something didn't want me to succeed, like there was a negative force stopping me. Self-doubt crept in, and I started to feel my purpose and drive slipping away. I felt like I was failing myself, because I thought that having a gift meant I would immediately become a radio personality. Since I hadn't, I thought that I was squandering the talent God had given me and that it was my fault.

I had to work at Marriott, Dollar Tree, and T.J. Maxx to make ends meet. I did have a job at a radio station because I was so hungry for my craft, but I wasn't doing the kind of work I was meant to be doing. I went on casting calls, trying out for dancing, acting, radio—anything and everything I could. I didn't know what was right, and everything I did made me feel worse. I got a job at a record label that I loved—I was doing admin work, and I got to go on the road with different artists . . . but then I got fired. That broke my heart, and I fell into a deep depression—but I didn't let anyone know I was hurting. I pasted on a smile that was so big it hid my pain, yet it never reached my eyes. It was the kind of smile we wear when we're posing for pictures—it's not real. It's devoid of genuine emotion, just there to make it seem like we're happy. My struggles were a silent battle that I fought on my own, and the pit of depression I fell into seemed so deep and dark I didn't know how I would ever crawl out of it.

I did get out, eventually, by finding a way to be all right with the stillness. It took a long time and a lot of patience, but if I hadn't made my peace with the silence, I would probably still be there now—because it was only when I was quiet that I could hear God again. I fell back from my friends, from a guy I liked, from going to the club and all the things I enjoyed . . . and that's how I began to rebuild my faith.

In the hush of that solitude, I understood this truth: *A delay is not a denial.* I came to understand that my journey toward my purpose was not meant to be a smooth, unobstructed path. It required effort, resilience, and the strength to persevere. I had to *work* to get to my purpose; it's not supposed to come easily.

That's a hard thing to realize, especially when you're young and full of dreams like I was. I thought, *God gave me this gift; shouldn't I get to use it?* And the answer is yes . . . but if I didn't have to work for it, I wouldn't have learned how to hone it. I wouldn't have cultivated the discipline and skill I have now that have made me so successful today. Sometimes I get asked about my faith, about how I know in my heart that God is real. My response is simple: I know God is real because I'm not where I once was. My transformation from despair to victory is a testament to divine presence in my life. Through the trials and tribulations, through the silence and solitude, I discovered the enduring strength of faith and the unwavering promise that a delay is merely a stepping stone toward the realization of my true purpose.

## Wild 'N Out

So how did I get here from there? I got up out of that hole, and I *worked*. I understood that I got fired from that record label job because as much as I was enjoying it, it wasn't helping me on the road to my purpose. Since it wasn't serving me, God made me uncomfortable so that I had to move into what I was supposed to be doing. I got active on social media and intensified my commitment to my comedy, honing my craft, and went back to working odd jobs just to get by while relentlessly pursuing my dreams.

And then, in 2016, something extraordinary happened. I made a video of a skit where I fight myself in the street, and it took the internet by storm, spreading like wildfire. A real-life viral moment.

Of course, that didn't mean it was making me any money! I could hear my dad's voice in my mind, asking, "How is this paying for a roof over your head?" But I had faith in myself now, and I knew I had to keep going. My best friend, Anika Anderson, pushed me, saying, "You can't stop there; you gotta keep going! What are you gonna do next?" I said, "Girl, I gotta create these characters now! I've been carrying them for so long."

All the characters I play now I developed by watching the people I grew up with—my mom yelling at us so passionately, my aunt arguing in her Jamaican accent, parents in the hood calling their kids "peanut" . . . My upbringing was the source of these characters, ultimately leading to my first brand deal with a hair company, and I started making five hundred dollars a month. It wasn't much, but it was something I could live off of for a while.

I continued to invest in myself. In 2017, I used some of my small savings to head down to Atlanta to create content that I'd later use to audition for *Wild 'N Out*, a sketch comedy, rap battle, improv game show series. I was nervous, and my friends were like, "Lie and say you got these connections! Say D.C. Young Fly is your cousin!" Well, I got into the audition, and they said I was funny . . . but when I looked for the email saying I'd made it, it never came.

Two years earlier, that would have been enough to send me spiraling back into that dark hole—but this time I knew better. I held on to my faith, and I remembered that *a delay is not a denial.* I returned to the grind, expanding my fan base and refining my craft. I got funnier, I lifted my prayer life, and I fortified my faith, because I knew this was just another instance of God making me uncomfortable so I would push myself to use my gift.

And then in 2018, it finally happened. The producers at *Wild 'N Out* reached out and told me they'd been watching me since my audition the year before. They said, "We see your numbers have grown, and you're working on your imaging . . . Would you like to come on the show?"

I've been on *Wild 'N Out* for nine seasons now. God brought that favor to me, and I took it and ran with it, gave it everything I had in me.

Of course, that first season, I was terrified! I thought maybe I'd get sent home immediately. I didn't know whether they liked me for me, for being a funny person, for my followers—or maybe for none of the above! I believed I was on the right track, but as I walked into that building, I felt all my confidence drain away. I knew I had to prove to them that I could bring to the stage what I was already doing on social media. This was my big break, and I was *not* going to waste it.

I practiced relentlessly. As soon as I went offstage and got back to the hotel, I practiced. I practiced in my dressing room. I had days when I didn't feel like I knew myself onstage or offstage, because I was in one character or another every moment of every day. It was exhausting and exhilarating, and even though I was nervous and scared, I was also filled with energy because I *knew* I was where I was supposed to be, finally doing what I was supposed to do.

The most incredible thing Nick Cannon ever told me was, "You are here for a reason. You are a star."

And I knew that was true. It was my mama's prophecy all over again; she's the one who said, "You're going to be in the arts. You're going to be a star." I had to fight to get where I am today. I had to get into my faith and learn how to believe in myself wholeheartedly. I had to learn how to let God lead and to not depend on others for anything, because as much as we love people, they will fail us from time to time. I had to learn how to do the work myself, knowing that my gift and what I had to offer the world were worth every ounce of effort and perseverance.

## Let's Talk About Faith

Faith, for me, has always been synonymous with Jesus Christ, a belief deeply rooted in my upbringing by pastors. I believe that faith will give you an unwavering trust in your purpose, in the idea that each one of us was meant for something unique and significant in this world. Faith will provide healing during the tough times.

Because there will be tough times. I can promise you that! The only way for you to remember that a delay is not a denial is to hold fast to your faith. When you seek and strive yet your dreams don't come to you the moment you think they should, take a step back and ask yourself, *Am I in alignment with my purpose?* If your answer is yes, then this delay is merely a detour and your dreams will find their way to you through a different route. However, if your pursuits aren't aligned with your values and your true purpose, then you're headed in the wrong direction.

Your values are the beliefs and principles that reside deep within your heart, guiding you toward what is right both for yourself and for the world. I've turned down so many opportunities and gigs because they weren't right for me or didn't align with my standards or my identity as Pretty Vee. If it doesn't have my essence in it, I'm going to turn it down in a heartbeat. Your path to success is guided by your values, your authenticity, and your unique voice. Don't be afraid to stand on what you know. Don't shift away from your path even if someone else tells you to go a different way—because your values, your standards, and your image are important. What you believe is important.

When I reflect on values, I can't help but think of Mr. Daniels and his life dedicated to service. He taught me that every positive action we take, whether it's a shared laugh or a kind word, has a ripple effect on the world. And he guided me toward the understanding that a helping hand can be the greatest gift you can give. Our assignments on this earth, the blessings and gifts we've been endowed with, are not solely meant for our benefit. My gifts are not just for me. When I make people laugh, I am healing them, as laughter and comedy have a remarkable ability to mend our souls and allow us to express ourselves freely.

I'm an all-purpose entertainer, and as I'm onstage in front of people and doing my characters, something amazing happens—I become a conduit for healing, both for the people watching me and for myself. Through my characters and performances, I offer them laughter, and in return, their laughter fills me with joy. It's a profound symbiotic experience, one that I believe can only occur if our lives are deeply aligned with our purposes. When I speak, I heal my inner child, and as I write this book, I am healing myself once more. This act of sharing, of passing on what I've learned and what I hold dear, is another act of service.

Service is not always monetary. Sometimes it's offering a word of encouragement or showing what courage, healing, or love looks like. Living your life authentically, celebrating your unique beauty and bravery, and standing proud in your Pretty Victory are themselves acts of service. You are an inspiration to others, demonstrating what it means to be unapologetically yourself.

# How to Reach Your Pretty Victory

I won't lie to you: These hundred days are not going to be easy. You'll have to delve deep inside yourself, explore your childhood, confront your fears, and unearth the things that have kept you silent and stagnant. Throughout this transformative process, you'll need to take an inventory of your values and truths. This is the place from which you'll draw strength and faith as you go through the process to reach what has been promised to you.

I think some people look at my life and think, *Wow, check out Pretty Vee; she got so successful overnight,* as if somebody put me in a microwave like a bag of popcorn and out popped a snack. But you know the truth behind that—I had to *work* for it. The world knows me, but they don't know this part of me. All they get is the comedic side of Vee, but you know that I had to go through my own process to reach my promise and create my own victories. This book is going to give you the recipe so you can do it too.

And when these hundred days are over? You'll be addicted to miracles, to hope, and, most importantly, to the taste of victory. You're going to know in your heart that brokenness doesn't last forever. Your soul will have been fed with a daily dose of confidence, and through this journey, you'll not only discover healing but also uncover the path to your purpose.

My vision for this book is so much more than a bunch of pages of paper. It's bringing forth an army of readers who have become pretty and victorious. I hope you'll go on to create your own harmonious cycle of giving and receiving, sharing your unique gifts with the world in service, and finding your own healing in the process. Together, we will forge a path toward a beautiful, more victorious future.

# 100 DAYS
*to* Your
Pretty Victory

# DAY ONE

## Stay Present in Your Blessings!

I started in the entertainment industry in 2016. I was doing funny skits on social media, working for my big break. I didn't want to be left behind, so I pushed myself to be the hardest-working woman in the room. I didn't take a break, ever . . . until the headaches and exhaustion came and I had to sit down. Then I settled into a moment of reflection, embracing the stillness and allowing myself to truly appreciate my accomplishments.

Most of the time, life pushes us from one task to the next. It's a perpetual cycle of doing, doing, doing without ever taking a moment to simply sit and relish our blessings. We get so caught up in the hustle that we forget to look around and be grateful for what we already have and what we've already accomplished.

Stop stressing! I'm talking to *you*, the person who is reading this right now. Stop trying to move so fast—you can move at your own pace. Trust me, I've been there, and I missed many great moments because I wanted to keep working instead of appreciating what I had. Tomorrow isn't going anywhere—all those tasks will get done. You need to find stillness *today*.

The next time you achieve something, no matter how big

or small, pause and savor it! Give yourself a well-deserved high five, and bask in the glow of your accomplishment, reveling in the joy that brings. These are the moments that make life meaningful, and they deserve to be cherished and celebrated. Life is not just a series of tasks to be completed; it's a collection of moments to be experienced, savored, and remembered. Your hard work deserves a seat at the table of your blessings.

## Time to Write It Out

*In this moment, release your thoughts on being present in your blessings.*

........................................................................................

........................................................................................

........................................................................................

........................................................................................

........................................................................................

........................................................................................

........................................................................................

........................................................................................

........................................................................................

........................................................................................

........................................................................................

........................................................................................

*Pretty Prayer*

**Do it for them, Jesus. Period.**

## DAY TWO

# A Delay Is Never a Denial!

D on't you hate the words *not now*? Don't you hate a "We'll see," a "Maybe someday," a "Check back with us at a later date"?

These delays feel like denial. They feel like rejection, like closed doors with no hope of other ways in. But just because they *feel* that way doesn't mean they *are* that way.

When I first auditioned for *Wild 'N Out*, I went all the way to New York City with no money whatsoever and no idea what to expect. I was so excited, but I didn't really have any material—all I had were a few skits I was doing on social media. I just showed up, knowing that I had the gift of comedy inside me . . . and as I mentioned before, I got rejected. I thought that was a closed door—but it wasn't, because the following year, they reached out to me again, and that time I *did* get on.

I have been told no so many times, have faced countless rejections. But each one served as a spark of motivation, pushing me to keep going. To achieve your dreams, your purpose has to be like a fire that burns brighter in the face of adversity, propelling you to work harder, dream bigger, and strive for excellence.

We all encounter moments when we hear that two-letter word: *no*. It can be disheartening, discouraging, and even soul-crushing at times. But here's the secret that refueled my resilience and determination: *No* is not the end of the road; it's just a detour. It's a temporary delay.

I want you to imagine the path that leads toward your dreams—it's filled with twists, turns, and unexpected obstacles. Sometimes, usually when you least expect it, a *no* sign appears, forcing you to stop, like a red light. But it doesn't mean you gotta turn around and go back! It's just a pause, a brief delay in your journey, a moment to catch your breath, reassess your route, and gather the strength you need to keep going forward.

## Time to Write It Out
*In this moment, release your thoughts on*
*getting through the delays.*

........................................................................................

........................................................................................

........................................................................................

........................................................................................

........................................................................................

........................................................................................

........................................................................................

........................................................................................

*Pretty Prayer*

**Your blessings will come when it's your season!**

# It's Human to Be Afraid of the Unknown

I had anxiety when I got out of college. I was afraid of the what-ifs and the maybes, afraid of not immediately getting a radio job. Afraid of the unknown. Fear gripped my heart and got ahold of me. I thought I would be the next big thing in radio . . . but no job interviews happened. I had no referrals, no contacts.

Everyone faces a season where they are scared to step out. But I'm here to tell you that your fear does *not* have control of you. It's okay to be afraid. You *don't* know what's going to happen next. But here I am, screaming that it's time to put that fear aside! This is your season for success, and you are going to get whatever your heart desires.

So let's take a look at your anxiety. Maybe you've been doubting your abilities or your gifts. Maybe you've been questioning whether you've really got what it takes or are ready to take the next steps. But I am here to tell you that you've got this! You are *more* than capable, and this, right now, is your time. It's true that anxiety is a tough enemy—but it's not invincible. You have the power to overcome it, to rise above its whispers of doubt, and to reclaim your season of victory.

Don't stay stuck, and don't allow the spirit of anxiety and

depression to overtake you. God has the last say-so. Don't allow the negative thoughts to steal your season of victory. They are like weeds that can choke your growth and cut you off from your purpose. Get rid of them. When you catch yourself looking back on past roadblocks and delays, remember—they were there to push you onward. Keep going, plant your feet where they need to be, and keep your eyes on the path ahead. This is your season to step out and seize everything your heart desires. Let your anxiety be the fuel that propels you forward, not the anchor holding you back. Just walk into your victory with a fresh pair of Jordans or YSL shoes on. Y'all are going to be all right. I believe in you.

## Time to Write It Out

*In this moment, release your fears and anxieties.*
*What is holding you back?*

........................................................................................

........................................................................................

........................................................................................

........................................................................................

........................................................................................

........................................................................................

........................................................................................

*Pretty Prayer*

**Step out! There's a blessing with your name on it!**

# Why Are You Giving Up?

S ometimes other people will give up on you.

It's painful, but it happens. It could even be someone you love and trust. Maybe it comes from a place of love, and they think they're doing what's best for you. They might think, *This dream is not realistic. It's not smart. It's just going to lead to pain and disappointment.* They're out there trying to protect you, not realizing that they're hurting you instead.

When that happens, you gotta remember to keep having faith in yourself. Your journey is *yours*, not theirs. Your path to success might not align with the expectations or understanding of those around you—but that doesn't matter. You are valuable, cherished, and deserving of all the good that life has to offer.

That doesn't mean that things will always go your way. You might not get that promotion, or maybe your current job doesn't align with your true passions and aspirations. Don't let these setbacks deter you from your path. Your worth is determined not by these points on a résumé alone but also by the resilience, determination, and unwavering faith you carry within you.

Consider this Pretty Truth: *In the midst of your shift, be still, because something greater is coming for you. Your life has a larger purpose, and your gifts won't be wasted. Don't give up.*

Remember, you are not alone on this path. There are people who believe in you, support you, and recognize your potential. *I* believe in you. Seek out those who uplift and inspire you.

## Time to Write It Out
*In this moment, what affirmations will help you stay determined?*

........................................................................................

........................................................................................

........................................................................................

........................................................................................

........................................................................................

........................................................................................

........................................................................................

........................................................................................

........................................................................................

........................................................................................

*Pretty Prayer*

**I know things won't always go right, but stay on this journey and keep your feet planted on this walk to greatness. Promise yourself that you won't give up!**

# I Have Been Told No
# So Many Times, but One Yes
# Changed My Life

Y ou're going to get told no a lot. That's just part of the process—that's how you're being guided to stay on the right path. Maybe if you hadn't gotten that no, you would have ended up doing something that wasn't right for you, and it would have meant a longer delay.

Now, I'm not saying no doesn't hurt to hear. It is *not* a fun word. But it's also not the end of the game. It doesn't mean that what you are striving for isn't going to happen for you. It's a test of your faith, to see if you'll keep on believing. It's a stepping stone on the path to your ultimate yes.

Sometimes, it only takes one yes. You can hear no after no after no, but that one little yes is all you need. Let me share a Pretty Truth: *They told me no. They told me I wasn't funny enough. But look at me now.* I heard no so many times— but that one yes that got me on *Wild 'N Out?* It was all I needed.

But here's the thing: That yes might take a long time, and you can't just sit around and wait for it to happen— that's not going to get you anywhere. You've got to keep working and hustling and striving, even when you're hearing no over and over. And how do you do that? *You be your own yes.*

Baby, don't you give up. Keep pushing forward. I challenge you to keep believing and keep going.

Your faith will be your yes.

## Time to Write It Out
*In this moment, how will you release their no?*

......................................................................................................
......................................................................................................
......................................................................................................
......................................................................................................
......................................................................................................
......................................................................................................
......................................................................................................
......................................................................................................
......................................................................................................
......................................................................................................
......................................................................................................
......................................................................................................

*Pretty Prayer*

**Yes. Your purpose is activated.
Hustlers don't stop; we keep going!**

# DAY SIX

## Start *You* Again

I t's never too late.

If you're reading this and thinking, *If only I'd started sooner . . .* or *I had my chance already and I missed it*, then I'm here to tell you this: *You're not dead.*

If you're alive, then you have the opportunity to truly *live* again.

So get out of your chair! Quit sitting around making excuses for why you can't do it now, when *now* is exactly the right time for you. Now is when you were always supposed to do this, because this moment right here, this is where your path has led you.

But you have to take the next steps. You have to say, "I am the only one living my life. I get to decide what I want to do with it." If you just keep sitting around lamenting missed opportunities, then you'll just keep missing them. Your own life is going to pass you by.

It's *never* too late to choose yourself. As long as you have breath in your lungs, you possess the incredible opportunity to embrace life fully once more. You are the sole architect of your life, and you need to go out and pursue your dreams *right now,* this very moment. This is precisely the right time for you.

# Time to Write It Out

*In this moment, how will you get up and live as you?*

........................................................................

........................................................................

........................................................................

........................................................................

........................................................................

........................................................................

........................................................................

........................................................................

........................................................................

........................................................................

........................................................................

........................................................................

........................................................................

........................................................................

........................................................................

........................................................................

........................................................................

........................................................................

*Pretty Prayer*

**As long as you are alive, you can live for you.**

# You Can't Sit at My Table

One thing I've learned about working in the entertainment industry is this: Sometimes the people you think are your friends aren't. I had people who loved me one day, absolutely fawned over me, acting like I was the funniest thing out here. The next day, it was like I didn't even exist. It's a harsh reality, one I had to get used to in order to survive in this world.

I know that isn't unique to this business. We all have people in our lives who seem to love us one day and hate us the next. *Those people are not your friends.* They clothed themselves but left you naked. They ate, but you didn't get fed.

So let me ask you this: Why, if they come and knock at your door and ask to sit at your table, are you letting them take a seat? You have the right to sit in your seat and not let the next person come. You get to decide—you don't have to give it away to just anyone. It is perfectly okay not to share when your own cup isn't overflowing. If your cup is full and you have the capacity to give, then that's great—but that's not where you are right now.

This is your stingy season. Stop trying to rescue and help other people when *you* are not yet where *you're* supposed to be. You make sure you stay in your seat until you are full—only then will you give it up. For now, you go ahead and tell them, "How about you go make your own table? This one is mine. You can't sit here."

## Time to Write It Out

*In this moment, how will you fill your own cup first?*

........................................................................

........................................................................

........................................................................

........................................................................

........................................................................

........................................................................

........................................................................

........................................................................

........................................................................

........................................................................

........................................................................

........................................................................

........................................................................

........................................................................

........................................................................

*Pretty Prayer*

**This is your stingy season—tell them to move along!**

# There's a Process Before the Promise

We all have to go through some things. We're all going to have our trials and tribulations—no life can be lived without them, and more importantly, no dream can be reached without overcoming them.

It's like building a house. You don't just get some land and then the next day, *bam!*—there's your dream house. No, you've got to get the lot surveyed. You have to buy the building materials, hire some contractors, lay the foundation, build the framework, put up the drywall—all of that and more has to happen before you can move in. It's a process, filled with different stages of effort.

And that process is not always easy. It's going to require hard work. While your friends are all at the club, you might have to stay home, sitting alongside your unwavering faith. You might not always have fun along the way. You're gonna have to make sacrifices. You might even cry at night. *The process is hard—but the promise is rewarding.*

The promise is an answered prayer. I am *living* in an answered prayer, because I shed the blood, the sweat, the tears. I did all that hard work. I kept going even after I was rejected over and over—when I fell down, I got up and tried again, pushing myself through the process.

And when at last my promise came, I received peace. I live with love, joy, and so much wisdom. I don't have everything I want in life—I'm still striving—but I am no longer lacking. I have what my dad so badly wanted for me, financial stability from my purpose. I know I can succeed. And this is my promise to you: All you gotta do is get up and try again, and you'll get here too.

## Time to Write It Out

*In this moment, where are you in your process?*

..................................................................................................

..................................................................................................

..................................................................................................

..................................................................................................

..................................................................................................

..................................................................................................

..................................................................................................

..................................................................................................

..................................................................................................

..................................................................................................

*Pretty Prayer*

**The process is tough, but the promise is so rewarding.**

# DAY NINE

## Don't Let Your Gift Die

Being a Jamaican growing up in Miami, I watched my family get what they needed, be present in their lives, and give all of us, their children, what we wanted. But I also heard the stories: *If I had this, I would have traveled the world . . . been a doctor . . . been a lawyer . . .* And I always wondered, Why didn't they? What held them back? Why didn't they succeed? Why didn't they have the faith to go explore and get high off life?

And I think the answer is this: They were scared of the what-ifs, so they decided that what they had was good enough. All they knew was family and making sure that the household was together and that everyone had what they needed. Which is important—I would never say otherwise. But they let their own gifts and creativity fall by the wayside.

So hear me clear right now! Don't just settle for what life hands you—get married, have kids, and let your gifts fade away out of fear. My family members couldn't break out of their shells because of *fear.* They didn't feel like they had the capacity to go through the process. But you do, and to leave a place and journey to someplace new, you have to walk in faith. You have to allow yourself to be thrown into an un-familiar space where you have room to explore your gift.

The time is *right now*. This isn't something that only happens when you're young—new gifts arise all the time. Ask yourself, *What is my gift today?* Listen for the answer, move with it, and don't look back. You have the capacity. Let your gift shine so bright that you follow it, even if it leads you along a path that seems frightening at first.

## Time to Write It Out
*In this moment, what are you afraid of?*

......................................................................................................

......................................................................................................

......................................................................................................

......................................................................................................

......................................................................................................

......................................................................................................

......................................................................................................

......................................................................................................

......................................................................................................

......................................................................................................

......................................................................................................

......................................................................................................

*Pretty Prayer*

**Soar into your purpose–your gift will make room for you!**

# DAY TEN

## I Forgive You

I call forgiveness *victory healing.*

For a long time, I didn't understand what forgiveness was, and that lack of awareness showed up in all my relationships—with family, friends, romance, you name it. I didn't know what it was to truly let things go, to move on and be happy. There was always a part of me that held on and something in my heart that whispered, *I forgive you, but I'm not going to forget it.* I tell you what—that's not forgiveness. You're still holding it over that other person, and when you do that, you hold yourself back too.

Forgiveness is peace. From the time we are children, we experience so many traumas. And even when we get to a better understanding of these experiences and begin the journey to heal them, we still don't know how to let go and let God come in and help us get to a better place—because our bitterness keeps us from forgiving ourselves, let alone anyone else.

Forgiveness has to start with you, for only then can you truly forgive others and find peace. So how can you be healed? What steps can you take toward your victory healing?

The first person to apologize to is *you.* To forgive those

who hurt you, you need to forgive yourself. To move into your purpose, you have to move past your trauma. Don't let your trauma make a house inside you, and don't let fear hold you captive. Don't wait on someone else to pick up the phone and forgive you—do it yourself, for yourself. Let it go, truly.

## Time to Write It Out

*In this moment, how can you begin to forgive yourself?*

........................................................................................................

........................................................................................................

........................................................................................................

........................................................................................................

........................................................................................................

........................................................................................................

........................................................................................................

........................................................................................................

........................................................................................................

........................................................................................................

*Pretty Prayer*

**Let it go, and step into your victorious healing.**

# Sometimes Growth Requires Walking Alone

I used to surround myself with noise. I was so scared of being alone—I always wanted someone at my house, hanging out with me, and if nobody was there, I would talk to them on the phone or FaceTime. If I had to make an important call, I always wanted someone else to be on it with me, offering their support and input. I just felt better with someone else around.

But my mom used to tell me, "You've gotta go get quiet and alone so God can speak to you."

When I was at my lowest and my most depressed, I was alone a lot—but I wasn't quiet. I kept trying to drown out the negative thoughts in my mind with distractions, scrolling through social media, looking at this video, watching that, always trying to bring the world into the darkness with me so I didn't have to sit in my sadness. But the truth was, that distraction was keeping God *out*, and it was only when I let myself truly be alone and quiet that I found my way out of that darkness.

When we can't be alone with ourselves, we drown out not just God's voice but our own voices too. The noise of the world is a distraction, and it's disturbing to the spirit.

You've got to get quiet and sit in the silence—not the sadness—so you can hear your own truth.

So I challenge you today: Put your phone on Do Not Disturb. Walk this journey alone today, for at least an hour or two. I know it can be scary. I know you don't know where you'll end up. But growth requires walking alone to understand where you're called to be—otherwise, you're just walking in place.

## Time to Write It Out

*In this moment, how can you find quiet and turn off the noise?*

........................................................................................................

........................................................................................................

........................................................................................................

........................................................................................................

........................................................................................................

........................................................................................................

........................................................................................................

........................................................................................................

........................................................................................................

........................................................................................................

*Pretty Prayer*

**When you're alone, you can hear yourself.**

# DAY TWELVE

## Prayer

I grew up in the church, so I prayed—no ifs, ands, or buts about it. I remember getting on the bus with my cousins and going to hear people shouting their prayers and speaking in tongues, having their own time with God in their secret places. And I have to tell you, when I was little, I didn't really understand all that. But I have since come to understand what prayer means and that it really does work.

The truth is, prayer is simple: You go to God, and you tell Him what you need. He will read the tablets of your heart, and whatever you desire, He will give it—or something He knows is better.

It doesn't have to be traditional. You don't gotta get down on your knees and put your hands together—that's not what prayer is all about. It's about *being with God.* You can talk to Him in your car, at the bus stop, even while you're scrolling on Instagram. I don't care what space you're in; I don't care if you feel alone, if you need a new car, or if you need money to pay your mortgage—the God I serve can make those miracles happen.

But it may not happen in the way you expect. Faith comes with belief. You might not get that car right away, but if you're consistent at prayer, your prayer posture and your belief system will enhance. And you'll find yourself going, *Oh. I thought I would get money to buy a car, but instead my cousin gave me his old Lexus—and it's nicer than anything I could have bought myself.* That's what keeping the faith means.

Give God forty-five minutes of your time, and tell Him everything that's in your heart. He will shape it for you. Your blessings will overflow. You will feel so rejuvenated, and you will tell the enemy goodbye when he tries you (you know he will!) because you will have the armor of prayer around you. So regardless of where you are and what you're looking for, I promise you that the door you're supposed to walk through will open with prayer.

## Time to Write It Out
*In this moment, how will you pray?*

........................................................................................................

........................................................................................................

........................................................................................................

........................................................................................................

........................................................................................................

........................................................................................................

........................................................................................................

*Pretty Prayer*

**It's simple. Just talk to God . . . Now turn to the next page.**

# DAY THIRTEEN

## Fight Until You Win

Y ou're gonna lose sometimes. You're gonna fight as hard as you can—and then you're gonna go down fighting.

You're gonna work so hard on that application, put everything you have into it—and then they're gonna hire somebody else. You're gonna write a book, putting your whole heart in every page, and even though it's amazing, it's not gonna sell, because that's the way it goes sometimes.

Things like that will happen, and it's going to feel like a sign for you to give up. But *it's not*. It's a sign for you to keep trying, to keep fighting.

Remember, it's supposed to be hard. If it all came easy and you didn't have to work for it, you wouldn't be able to hone your skills, strengthen your faith and your values, and become the solid rock that *you yourself* can lean on when it gets tough—because I promise you, it always does. If it's not hard at the beginning, then it will be hard later.

Life is a roller coaster of ups and downs, and even when you give it your all, you can find yourself at the bottom. If it feels like the world is against you and you want to throw in the towel—baby, that's your sign to dig in even deeper and keep on fighting! Setbacks are only stepping stones that will lead you toward your ultimate success. Keep moving forward, keep fighting, because it's through those hardships that you'll discover your strength and reach your true potential.

## Time to Write It Out

*In this moment, how can you find the strength to keep fighting?*

...................................................................................................

...................................................................................................

...................................................................................................

...................................................................................................

...................................................................................................

...................................................................................................

...................................................................................................

...................................................................................................

...................................................................................................

...................................................................................................

...................................................................................................

...................................................................................................

*Pretty Prayer*

**You're gonna keep fighting, every day.**

# DAY FOURTEEN

## Choose New Thoughts

We all have inner dialogues, voices chattering in our minds saying we're not pretty enough, not strong enough, not capable enough. That we don't have what it takes. That our plans aren't going to work out. That we don't have the finances, that we're not qualified, that we'll always be stuck at the job we hate.

Those thoughts are always gonna come. But if you allow them to become something that feels true and right, you'll get enmeshed in them. You have to *expand* on those thoughts, twist them around on themselves. Ask God to change them. If you're thinking, *I'm not pretty enough . . .* you've got to add on *I am more beautiful than I know.*

*I'm not strong enough . . . I'm committed to doing what it takes.*

*I'll always be stuck in this same job . . . I'm going to do what I have to in order to set myself free. I'm not trapped.*

*My plans aren't going to work out . . . I will achieve what my heart desires.*

Change your thoughts to change your life. Make yourself magnetic to greatness. If you stay stuck in the same negative, always-gonna-lose thoughts, you'll never move forward. Nothing will ever change for you. Your same old routine is not going to bring anything new to your life. And the first step has to be changing how you think, because if you change your mindset, you can invite abundance and possibility into your life instead of all that limitation. Don't let those negative thoughts hold you back any longer. Challenge them, rewrite them, and watch as your life transforms before your eyes.

## Time to Write It Out

*In this moment, how will you challenge your negative thoughts?*

......................................................................................................

......................................................................................................

......................................................................................................

......................................................................................................

......................................................................................................

......................................................................................................

......................................................................................................

......................................................................................................

......................................................................................................

......................................................................................................

......................................................................................................

*Pretty Prayer*

**God, I ask that You give each of us a new way of thinking.**

# DAY FIFTEEN

## A Healthy Diet

You are what you consume. This is my motto, but I didn't understand what health meant for years. It took my mom looking like she's aging backward, like I'm looking at Benjamin Button every day, for me to ask her secret. Her answer: no stress!

I know you're thinking, *Oh sure, no problem. I'll just erase all my stress, like it's that easy.* No, it's not easy—and that's why what we feed our bodies and our minds is so important. We're talking a lot about what you put in your mind and how you gotta cancel out all those negative thoughts. It works the same with your body.

I know it's easier to buy that burger off the dollar menu, but your body deserves better than that. I've been hood vegan for years, and I feel so much more clarity and so much less stress. I've got more energy and positivity. (Yes, hood vegan—'cause I tap into some lamb chops and a little turkey bacon sometimes. It's not about being perfect; it's about being mindful of what I'm consuming.)

When you wake up in the morning, are you restless from not being able to sleep all night? Are you sluggish and cranky because you skipped the most important meal of the day? Are you finding it hard to complete everyday tasks while also staying active? If so, then it's time for a change! The things you put in your body can shape your well-being. What are you doing to feed your life as a whole? I changed my diet because I wanted to change my thoughts—and that's how I changed my life. If you want your brain right, you got to eat right.

## Time to Write It Out

*In this moment, how will you be more intentional about what you consume?*

........................................................................................

........................................................................................

........................................................................................

........................................................................................

........................................................................................

........................................................................................

........................................................................................

........................................................................................

........................................................................................

........................................................................................

*Pretty Prayer*

**Put that pork chop down, and go get on this hood vegan diet.**

# DAY SIXTEEN

## If You Look Good, You Feel Good

I gotta talk to my ladies now. How many of you are going to the grocery store looking like Holiday Heart? (No shade, ladies!)

I know some days you don't have the energy. I know it feels like you don't have the time, that you have too many responsibilities and too much running around to do to sit in that chair for a couple of hours and let somebody pamper your feet and do your hair. But don't you know that looking good and feeling good *give* you energy? Even with all that you have going on, you have to make time for *you*. Your appearance on the outside can impact how you feel on the inside. It can give you confidence.

And, guys, it's time to go get your hair cut, get that crisp line-up.

Ain't it crazy how good it makes you feel to look good? I used to be the girl in my house with no nails or toes or hair done—I didn't do any of that unless I had a booking, and only *then* did I get up and get myself looking good. But that wasn't for *me*—that was for everybody else. I deserve to look good and feel good just for myself! And you do too. So put on your makeup even if you know you're not gonna leave the house. Wear your good clothes. Baby, get up right now and get to the hair salon.

Besides, you never know when that phone's gonna ring! You never know how soon an opportunity will come knocking on your door. You'd better be ready when it does.

## Time to Write It Out

*In this moment, how will you get yourself looking good so you feel good?*

....................................................................................................

....................................................................................................

....................................................................................................

....................................................................................................

....................................................................................................

....................................................................................................

....................................................................................................

....................................................................................................

....................................................................................................

....................................................................................................

....................................................................................................

....................................................................................................

*Pretty Prayer*

**God, please, I pray my readers make it on time to their hair appointments. Because when you look good, you feel good.**

# DAY SEVENTEEN

## You're Slipping, Friend

All right, you've been at this for a little over two weeks now. How are you feeling? I bet you're settling into a bit of a routine, getting into the rhythm of it. You're starting to feel like maybe you've got this and you can relax a little bit.

Well, guess what: That means you're getting a little *too* comfy. You're not pushing yourself. You're not taking the initiative or daring yourself to try harder, to move beyond your comfort zone. It's time to challenge yourself and strive for more.

If you let this go on for too long, something's going to happen to make you push yourself out of your comfort zone. It'll dump you right out of your chair and make you scramble to find your feet. And when that happens, it's gonna hurt. So don't wait around for it! Get yourself up *now*, make yourself uncomfortable, and try harder. Push your own boundaries, stretch your limits, and strive for more than you've been allowing yourself to believe in.

It's just like working out. Once it starts feeling easy, that means you gotta step it up. You gotta increase the intensity, or you won't get any stronger—you'll just stay the same: stagnant and stuck. Don't settle for comfortable.

Seek growth, embrace discomfort, and continue to give it your all. This journey is about progress, and you've got the power to propel yourself forward. Keep pushing, keep striving, and you'll see just how far you can go.

## Time to Write It Out

*In this moment, where have you become too comfortable? Where can you push harder?*

.............................................................................................................................

.............................................................................................................................

.............................................................................................................................

.............................................................................................................................

.............................................................................................................................

.............................................................................................................................

.............................................................................................................................

.............................................................................................................................

.............................................................................................................................

.............................................................................................................................

.............................................................................................................................

.............................................................................................................................

.............................................................................................................................

*Pretty Prayer*

**If it's easy, you need to step it up.**

# DAY EIGHTEEN

## Don't Carry Your Pain Alone

A while ago, I was stuck in a relationship that was holding me back. I'd been in it for five years, and I didn't think I would ever get out. I didn't feel like I had control. I was being manipulated, and their conniving spirit had gotten all over me. I was in so much pain, and the worst of it was, I didn't even fully understand it. I thought that was love. I thought I was safe. I thought that since this other person was successful, I could curl up in *their* blessings, not knowing that I had to go looking for my own. Not knowing that I cannot be controlled.

All I knew was that I was hurting, and I didn't know why.

So I sat down in front of my mirror and said, "God, I need You to take this away from me. I need You to take this pain, take this frustration, take this confusion away from me." And He did.

Six months of soul-searching and praying went by, and at the end of that time, I felt so much lighter. With the weight of my pain lifted from my shoulders, I had the strength to gain my confidence back. And with that confidence, I broke myself out of that relationship. I didn't want to be around them anymore. I didn't want to suffer in that space, not for one minute longer.

But I could never have seen that if I hadn't allowed God to take my pain from me. Our suffering blocks our vision, and if we can't see where we're going, we will never move forward. Don't carry your pain alone, when you can just give it to God.

## Time to Write It Out

*In this moment, how will you give your pain to God?*

........................................................................................................

........................................................................................................

........................................................................................................

........................................................................................................

........................................................................................................

........................................................................................................

........................................................................................................

........................................................................................................

........................................................................................................

........................................................................................................

........................................................................................................

*Pretty Prayer*

***You'd better dump your problems, your pain, your worries, on God. Stop carrying that Walmart bag around. Keep going, and let's go!***

# DAY NINETEEN

## Follow God's Instructions

God gave you instructions—we are all given a distinct gift at birth, and it is up to us to nourish it! The trouble is, it can be hard to hear His wisdom, because we get caught up in asking for advice from our friends and family instead. You don't need to ask the people around you—God has given you the wisdom you need. God told you to leave your abusive husband. To quit your job. To stay in your hometown. But you didn't listen. God's instructions are plain and clear—yet sometimes we don't obey them, because we get caught up in what we want to do instead. We're shortsighted, distracted, and limited in our vision. God's instructions are limitless, and if we follow them, what we've got going on will last forever.

But we have to learn how to get quiet enough to hear Him. Finding stillness in a world that is perpetually in motion can help you connect with yourself, with your truth. You can recognize the abundance that already exists in your life, both tangible and intangible, in the people who love and support you, the opportunities that have come your way, and the experiences that have shaped you. In this stillness, you can tune in to God.

I know that at some point you lost the ability to hear Him and follow His instructions. That's okay—I've got you. You're reading this to get better, to get healed, so you'll remember to follow those directions the first time around.

## Time to Write It Out
*In this moment, how will you be still enough to hear God?*

..........................................................................................

..........................................................................................

..........................................................................................

..........................................................................................

..........................................................................................

..........................................................................................

..........................................................................................

..........................................................................................

..........................................................................................

..........................................................................................

..........................................................................................

..........................................................................................

..........................................................................................

*Pretty Prayer*

**Follow God's instructions, not yours. Your way is limited. It will never last.**

# DAY TWENTY

## I Love You

I love you. I love you. I love you.

We don't hear those words often enough. I grew up in a Caribbean household where life was very disciplined and very hard, and for the most part "I love you" was never spoken. My mother said it, and sometimes my father, but hardly anyone else outside of that. Yet I knew I was loved, because I had God with me. He would never leave me or forsake me.

But of course, it's nice to hear the words "I love you" from people! Maybe you didn't hear them enough either. And I wonder, Do you speak them enough? Have you ever said "I love you" to your friends? I know some of us have grown up in spaces where showing our feelings can feel taboo—I sure did. But let's make it more common, and here, I'll go first:

One . . . two . . . three . . . *I love you.*

Yes, you! The person who is reading this right now. I love you because you decided to come along on this journey with me. I love that you had enough faith in yourself to get this far. You are not just a reader to me—you are a beautiful human being, a creation of God, and you deserve to be loved. You have not been alone reading these pages, because I have been praying for you the whole way through.

*I love you.* Don't forget that! Sometimes that's all anybody needs to hear. So if you ever find yourself needing to feel loved, just come back to this page and let me remind you: *I love you.*

## Time to Write It Out

*In this moment, how will you open yourself up to love?*

.......................................................................................................

.......................................................................................................

.......................................................................................................

.......................................................................................................

.......................................................................................................

.......................................................................................................

.......................................................................................................

.......................................................................................................

.......................................................................................................

.......................................................................................................

.......................................................................................................

.......................................................................................................

.......................................................................................................

*Pretty Prayer*

**Now go tell someone else that you love them.**

## What Makes You Victorious?

*Sisssstererrr! My prayer life and knowing God's word to counter the ridiculous suggestions Satan presents to me!! Winning that battle is what makes me victorious. I'm most secure when I know I'm in God's will, which puts me in my dominating space—a winner.*

KIERRA SHEARD, gospel singer

*Setting a goal to build something and seeing it through to completion.*

ISSA RAE, actress, writer, producer, and director

*Loving life makes me victorious. Learning and [being] willing to grow and change with the seasons helps me become the woman I want to be. Opening my arms wide to what life has to offer makes me victorious. I am an open book. I give myself grace when I make mistakes and use them as lessons to become better. I simply want to be me and to be free, living life through love. Everything else will fall into place, and wherever life takes me, I will always be victorious.*

KARRUECHE TRAN, award-winning producer,
actress, and business owner

*My faith, my strength, the purity of my heart. The will to always want to improve, and my family and friends that support me.*

Shenseea, Grammy Award–nominated singer and songwriter

*Getting out of bed in the morning after ten days of Covid. To God be the glory.*

June Ambrose, award-winning stylist, fashion designer, show host, author, and creative director

*My soul . . . my intention . . . and my thirst to want to positively contribute to everything that comes in contact with me.*

BenDaDonnn, stand-up comedian, actor, musician, producer, and social media sensation

*Waking up in the A.M. Blessed, seeing another day. Growing from failure. Not giving up. Facing adversity. Living in my purpose. Listening. Learning. Growing. Being a great father. Having character even when no one is looking. Staying humbled. Less worrying.*

Desi Banks, comedian, actor, entrepreneur, and social media dynamo

# DAY TWENTY-ONE

## Give Yourself Grace

This is a message to all my creators out there: You got this.

I know sometimes it feels like you have to be perfect. It feels like everybody's expectations of you are so high—and I know that your expectations of *yourself* are the highest of all. You're meant for great things, right? So that must mean you can never make mistakes.

Wrong. *Everybody* makes mistakes. There is not a single perfect person in this world, and I thank God for that. Perfect people are boring—they aren't creative. Perfect people are static—they don't grow. Perfect people are rigid—they don't bend. You are wonderfully, beautifully imperfect, and that means you get to make mistakes and learn from them. And what you learn will make you more creative, more empowered, more flexible, and, most importantly, more compassionate. The grace that you learn to give yourself, you will be able to give to others.

When you grow as a person and learn from your mistakes, you are opening doors not just for yourself but for everyone in your life. You are setting an example for others, showing them that it is possible to be *proud* of the mistakes we have made—to say, "Well, at least I tried. It didn't work out, but I took a risk, and I learned from it, and it made me better." When you have that kind of compassion for yourself, you can be more forgiving of others when they disappoint you. If you give yourself grace, you'll be able to extend that grace to those around you.

If you're reading this, I want you to know that the grace that I hold in my heart I extend to you. I'm so proud of you. You're doing a beautiful job. Embrace your mistakes, learn from them, and keep moving forward. Your imperfections are what make you unique and beautiful, and they are the stepping stones on the path to your victory.

## Time to Write It Out
*In this moment, how can you give yourself grace?*

.................................................................................................................
.................................................................................................................
.................................................................................................................
.................................................................................................................
.................................................................................................................
.................................................................................................................
.................................................................................................................
.................................................................................................................
.................................................................................................................

*Pretty Prayer*

**You don't need to be perfect all the time.**

# DAY TWENTY-TWO

## No Excuses

I love to go hiking in the mountains of Georgia. I like to work out, to feel good and look good. I want to stay looking like I'm in my twenties. But one day I was out hiking, and I was kind of tired, going slow—and then I looked to the left and saw this old couple passing me. I'm younger than they are, I weigh 130 pounds, and they were marching past me like they'd just had three green juices, just power walking their way up. And let me tell you, I don't care how tired I was in that moment. I was like, "Hell naw! I'm going to walk my tiny body up this mountain!"

If they can do it, you can get up there. One of my cousins was born with no arms, and I watched her drive, get active, graduate from college. She just got up and did it.

If you're feeling overwhelmed, tired, and lazy and like you can't achieve your goal? I don't care. No excuses. If it hits two o'clock in the afternoon and you're still in bed? Get up. Get to it and get active. Go be fit. You know you can do it. It's your mind that has to change, that's all. You go get yourself up that mountain. It's not just about physical fitness—it's about overcoming obstacles and pushing past your limitations. You have the power to rise above it all. So go ahead—go be victorious. The path may be steep, but with each step forward, you move closer to your victory.

## Time to Write It Out

*In this moment, how will you get up and get out?*

........................................................................................

........................................................................................

........................................................................................

........................................................................................

........................................................................................

........................................................................................

........................................................................................

........................................................................................

........................................................................................

........................................................................................

........................................................................................

........................................................................................

........................................................................................

........................................................................................

*Pretty Prayer*

**Your blessing is at the top of that mountain.
Are you gonna go get it?**

# DAY TWENTY-THREE

## Get Back to You

If you're feeling lost in the struggle, like everything has gotten a little too hard and you've lost the joy in what you're doing—that's a clear sign that it's time to get back to your happy place.

Sometimes we forget that there's more to life than work! It's easy to get caught up in doing, doing, doing, believing that constant effort is the key to achieving our goals. We take everything so seriously that we forget that life is supposed to be fun. We forget to actually live, to savor the moments, and to relish the simple pleasures that make life beautiful.

So take a moment to yourself, breathe in the fresh air, and allow yourself to exist in an authentic way that soothes you. Let the rustling leaves of the trees overhead calm you. Take some time to walk throughout the day—remember, it's okay to walk before you run! Feel God's light shining on your face from the sun, and feel the cool whispers of the wind providing you with reassurance. I know you're determined to grind no matter what, and I see all the work you have to do. But don't let that be *all* of you. Your life is yours to live, and you hold the key to your happiness—so don't let the stress of the world have authority over you!

Every day, and especially today, take the time to release the stress that settles into your life. Remind yourself that you are allowed to experience joy, and bask in the simple pleasures. That way, when you go back to work, you'll do so with a refreshed spirit and a heart filled with gratitude for the beauty of life. So go ahead and rediscover your happy place—it's always there for you.

## Time to Write It Out
*In this moment, how will you take the time to find joy and pleasure?*

........................................................................................................

........................................................................................................

........................................................................................................

........................................................................................................

........................................................................................................

........................................................................................................

........................................................................................................

........................................................................................................

........................................................................................................

........................................................................................................

........................................................................................................

*Pretty Prayer*

**Get your life back, friend!**

# DAY TWENTY-FOUR

## Have Faith and Keep Going!

I often think of doubt as getting a cold. Like "Oh, here we go. I gotta deal with this now." It's annoying and it slows me down and I have to push through it—but it's okay, because I know I'm going to overcome it.

Tell me if this sounds like you: You're up and down about your own abilities, where one day you're on top of the world, feeling like you're absolutely fantastic about what you do, and everything seems marvelous . . . but the next day, you want to crawl into a hole because you're convinced that everything you touch turns to dust. You can't complete a task because it feels like there's no point to it—it's not going to come to anything anyway. You have a bunch of brilliant ideas on a notepad, but you don't move them off the piece of paper and into reality because you feel like they aren't worthwhile. You're not seeing your own vision for what it is.

If that's you, it sounds like you've caught doubt. That's all right—it comes to everyone. Like a cold or flu, it makes its way around, and we all suffer from it sometimes.

What matters isn't whether you feel doubt; it's whether you let it stop you. You've got to trust your own abilities and your process, you've got to trust God, and you've got to go out there and do it, *even when you feel doubt*. Doubt may be a regular visitor, but it doesn't have to define you. It's a challenge to overcome, a hurdle to clear, and a test of your determination—so when it drops by, just have faith and keep going.

## Time to Write It Out
*In this moment, how will you keep the faith when you feel doubt?*

........................................................................................................

........................................................................................................

........................................................................................................

........................................................................................................

........................................................................................................

........................................................................................................

........................................................................................................

........................................................................................................

........................................................................................................

........................................................................................................

........................................................................................................

........................................................................................................

........................................................................................................

........................................................................................................

*Pretty Prayer*

**Doubt is just dropping by; it's not here to stay.**

# Why Hate on Me?

I get confused when people hate on me—I genuinely don't get it. I am an example of what's possible if you work hard and have faith . . . but I still get haters.

Before I was successful, I was motivated by the successes of others. If I saw somebody making it big on social media, onstage, on-screen, I thought, *Hey, good for them* and *That's gonna be me someday.* Their success gave me hope. My thinking is, if my peers are doing well, that means I can do well. If somebody gets a million dollars, that means I can get two million.

So why does my success make people want to come at me? What makes them feel that way?

All I can figure is, they are struggling with their own doubts and challenges, and they're not yet in a place where they can do the inner work they need to find their own success—so they are trying to pull me down instead of raising themselves up. There are a lot of people like that, and I hold so much compassion for them, because I know that it comes from a place of pain and suffering. You're going to encounter them, too, as you begin to reach your own successes. Sometimes it will feel like the people who are supposed to be your friends don't want you to achieve your dreams—and maybe that will even be true. They might be afraid you'll leave them behind. Maybe you'll have to someday.

For now, recognize that it isn't about you. *You* are working toward your promise.

## Time to Write It Out

*In this moment, how will you hold true to yourself when others try to keep you down?*

.......................................................................................

.......................................................................................

.......................................................................................

.......................................................................................

.......................................................................................

.......................................................................................

.......................................................................................

.......................................................................................

.......................................................................................

.......................................................................................

.......................................................................................

*Pretty Prayer*

**Why you hating on me? You just delaying your own blessings! Stay focused!**

# DAY TWENTY-SIX

# Keep Your Feet on the Ground

If your feet are planted firmly on the ground, you're less likely to get lost in the clouds of uncertainty and distraction.

Sometimes we lose focus—it happens to everybody. We find ourselves drifting, making plans but not following through, having these big ideas that never quite develop into anything concrete and actionable. We get sidetracked, caught up in little diversions that don't really further our goals.

That's fine. It's good to take breaks. It's good to get out and enjoy yourself. But make sure that's what those distractions are—enjoyable little breaks—and not you settling for second best or plan B or getting distracted by somebody else's advice or whatever shiny new idea comes your way.

That won't get you to your promise. All those distractions and deviations won't move you further along in your process. You gotta keep your motion going. Put your feet on the ground, and keep taking step after step—each one is a deliberate movement toward your ultimate goal. It's all about tackling one task at a time, like carefully stepping from one rock to another over a rushing river, each one bringing you closer to your destination.

# Time to Write It Out
*In this moment, how will you stay grounded?*

........................................................................................................
........................................................................................................
........................................................................................................
........................................................................................................
........................................................................................................
........................................................................................................
........................................................................................................
........................................................................................................
........................................................................................................
........................................................................................................
........................................................................................................
........................................................................................................
........................................................................................................
........................................................................................................
........................................................................................................
........................................................................................................
........................................................................................................
........................................................................................................
........................................................................................................
........................................................................................................

*Pretty Prayer*

**Each step brings you closer to your promise.**

# DAY TWENTY-SEVEN

## Secret Place

Your secret place is the location of the relationship between you and God.

It doesn't have to be anything fancy. For some people, it means going to church or creating an altar. But it can also be in your closet, your car, your bedroom—all it needs to be is a place where you can cut out the noise and be alone with God. We all have to find it for ourselves, carve it out in our lives, make space for it. You have to build that altar within so that wherever your secret place is, you can really and truly release there.

We move and are on the go so much, and we carry *so much* with us. We need to have a place where we can stop, be still, and put down our burdens. Where are you going to do all that?

It's a very intimate and powerful experience, and believe me, it feels *so good* that at times you won't even want to leave that secret place! Make sure you set aside some time every day to be still, to gather understanding and wisdom.

You've got to find that place in your home and in yourself. You have to find time to give God those moments alone with you. That's when you can empty yourself of all you've been carrying and then be filled up with all you need so you are ready to get on with the next part of your day, your week, your month, your life.

## Time to Write It Out
*In this moment, ask yourself,* Where is my secret place?

-------------------------------------------------------------

-------------------------------------------------------------

-------------------------------------------------------------

-------------------------------------------------------------

-------------------------------------------------------------

-------------------------------------------------------------

-------------------------------------------------------------

-------------------------------------------------------------

-------------------------------------------------------------

-------------------------------------------------------------

-------------------------------------------------------------

-------------------------------------------------------------

-------------------------------------------------------------

*Pretty Prayer*

**Put your phone on Do Not Disturb.
You're talking to God right now.**

# Check on Your Strong Friends

When I say "strong friends," you know the ones I'm talking about, right? The friends you call if you just want to laugh or go out for lunch with somebody who is always up for it. The ones who have it together, ready to conquer the world. The ones you can rely on, who always have a shoulder for you to cry on and a box of tissues handy. They're breaking down doors, winning big, striving and succeeding, and doing it all with smiles on their faces.

But those smiles? They're not always the real thing. Many times it's the kind of smile they paste on to hide what they're really feeling. I know that when I was struggling, some days my own smile would be even bigger than my pain, because I didn't want anyone to know what was going on inside. This is something we've been trained to do—by our childhoods, by societal expectations, and by our perceived need to protect those around us from our emotions and traumas. It's hard for us to share what we're really feeling.

But you know that you *love* your friend. So even if you think they're okay—reach out anyway. Ask them how they are. They need to know that you're there for them, that you believe in them, and that it's okay to not be okay for a little while. Because you are one of those strong friends too. And when you make a habit of checking in on others, you learn to do the same for yourself. The faith and support you extend outward can be a source of inward strength and self-compassion. So reach out to your friends, let them know you care, and remember that you, too, deserve the same love and support. The faith you have in others will become faith you can give to yourself.

## Time to Write It Out

*In this moment, which strong friends will you reach out to?*

......................................................................................................

......................................................................................................

......................................................................................................

......................................................................................................

......................................................................................................

......................................................................................................

......................................................................................................

......................................................................................................

......................................................................................................

......................................................................................................

*Pretty Prayer*

**Your true friends love and support you, and you love
and support them.**

# Get Out of Your Poverty Mindset

Y ou are capable of being rich.

And I'm not just talking about your bank account. I'm talking about being rich in every aspect of your life—rich in spirit, friendship, creativity, love, joy, and faith.

When I was growing up, my family had enough to get by and live pretty comfortably, but not everyone around me did. I saw what it was to be poor, and I knew I never wanted to feel that way. I didn't want to be stuck in the place where some of my friends were, because I understood something they didn't . . . that it wasn't just about the money. Their mindset was that poverty was all they had—that without a full wallet, they couldn't have a full heart or a curious mind.

I wanted my mind to be involved with great ideas and inventions. I wanted my heart to be full of love for the people around me. I wanted to explore everything the world had to offer, and I wanted to share all the gifts that God gave me.

And hell yes, I wanted the money that goes along with that.

To achieve all that, you have to get rid of all the dirt that clutters up your mind, discarding your limiting beliefs. You've got to clean yourself out, take that mindset to the trash, and give yourself a new one: that you are already rich. You have so much wealth—not just in money but also in wisdom, creativity, and love. If you embrace this new mindset, you'll discover the richness that has been inside you all along.

## Time to Write It Out

*In this moment, how will you empty out the trash of your mind?*

........................................................................................................

........................................................................................................

........................................................................................................

........................................................................................................

........................................................................................................

........................................................................................................

........................................................................................................

........................................................................................................

........................................................................................................

........................................................................................................

........................................................................................................

........................................................................................................

........................................................................................................

*Pretty Prayer*

**You are already rich in your gifts.**

# DAY THIRTY

# Change Your Fragrance and Change Your Language

I've had to let go of some people along the way. Sometimes I had to make the choice, while other times we just drifted apart. But guess what . . . it happens! As I began to work on myself and take the necessary steps toward my success, those friends and I didn't have the same conversations. We didn't speak the same language. We didn't talk the same way. Even our fragrance began to change. The things they used I didn't use. I had been rewired for a greater purpose, and those things became unfamiliar. I didn't have the capacity to step into that mode anymore.

I had changed, and they hadn't . . . so we eventually stopped hanging out, because we didn't have much to say to one another. That's one type of letting go, where you just kind of allow each other to go your separate ways, and it's okay.

But other times, the people who didn't change weren't okay with how I *had* changed. I'd started to move up in the world, and they didn't want me to go any higher. It made them feel frustrated since they weren't working on themselves, yet instead of deciding to make a change—or letting me do my own thing—they tried to get me to stay down. They tried to pull me back into doing the things I didn't want to do anymore, speaking the old language from the old mindset.

I can't be around people who don't want me to go higher. That's not real friendship. That's not wanting what's best for *me;* that's keeping me stuck so they can feel better about themselves. You're going to encounter people like that, too—people who aren't ready to go with you to your next level—so you might have to give up some relationships. That's okay. You're going to find the people who really love and support you.

## Time to Write It Out

*In this moment, how will you figure out which relationships are helping you move forward?*

........................................................................................................

........................................................................................................

........................................................................................................

........................................................................................................

........................................................................................................

........................................................................................................

........................................................................................................

........................................................................................................

*Pretty Prayer*

**Sometimes you have to move things around to get to your purpose.**

# DAY THIRTY-ONE

# The Bigger the Dream, the Harder the Grind

If your dream is to be famous, you're going to have to pound the pavement to make it big. If your dream is to be the best, you'll have to strive harder than everybody else, constantly pushing boundaries. If your dream is to stand in glory, then you will have to climb higher than anyone else has ventured before.

If that sounds tough, believe me—it is. I've worked tirelessly to get to where I am today, and I'm not finished yet. My dream is not fulfilled. There's more that I want to do in this life. I'm not done growing or achieving. I'm still cooking. Every time I succeed at something, make one of my dreams come true, I pick a new dream, plan out my next goal.

And what I've learned is that the bigger my dream is, the harder I have to work to make it come true.

Some people might tell you to start with a small dream, to give yourself a little success and then grow from there. And that's true—that can absolutely get you started. But here's my Pretty Truth: *Dream big, baby. Dream as big as your heart desires, and then let all those smaller dreams along the way serve as rungs on a ladder that you climb toward your ultimate goal.* Because it's the big dream that will make you work hard, put in your everything, and pour out your heart and soul to make the impossible possible. Keep climbing to greatness, one dream at a time.

## Time to Write It Out

*In this moment, what are your biggest dreams?*

........................................................................................................

........................................................................................................

........................................................................................................

........................................................................................................

........................................................................................................

........................................................................................................

........................................................................................................

........................................................................................................

........................................................................................................

........................................................................................................

........................................................................................................

........................................................................................................

........................................................................................................

........................................................................................................

........................................................................................................

*Pretty Prayer*

**You deserve your biggest dream!**

# DAY THIRTY-TWO

# Giving Up Isn't an Option

L et me tell you something about fallback plans.

I never let myself have one. Trust me and believe, I had day jobs and ways to make ends meet while I worked through my process. But I never let myself think about a secondary career or what I might do if I wasn't successful, if I didn't achieve my dream and fulfill my promise.

Here's the thing: When you allow yourself to contemplate the possibility of failure, entertaining the notion that you might not succeed, you are sowing the seeds of self-doubt and hesitation. You are prophesying, telling yourself that you will fail. If you give yourself an escape route, an easy way out, you'll be more likely to take it when the going gets tough.

You cannot give yourself that option. You cannot allow yourself to give up. Success requires a relentless pursuit of your dreams.

It's not about ignoring the possibility of failure; it's about refusing to accept it as a final outcome. Baby, you do *not* accept defeat as an option. By eliminating fallback plans, you force yourself to push through obstacles with unwavering determination.

So remember this: You cannot give yourself the luxury of an exit strategy. You cannot allow yourself to entertain the thought of giving up. Success requires an all-or-nothing mindset, and when you commit wholeheartedly to your dreams, failure becomes just a temporary setback on the path to your ultimate victory.

## Time to Write It Out
*In this moment, how will you renew your commitment?*

..............................................................................................
..............................................................................................
..............................................................................................
..............................................................................................
..............................................................................................
..............................................................................................
..............................................................................................
..............................................................................................
..............................................................................................
..............................................................................................
..............................................................................................
..............................................................................................
..............................................................................................

*Pretty Prayer*

**A *failure* is just a *setback*.**

# If You're Starving, You'll Eat Anything

When I was first starting out, I thought I had to take whatever came my way. I took a job at a record label even though, deep down, I knew it wasn't moving me toward my promise. But at that point, I thought, *Hey, hey, at least it's in the entertainment industry, so it must be a good thing, right?*

Wrong. I was starving. I was taking crumbs and letting those crumbs lead me off my path.

You have to trust in yourself. Trust in your promise, and trust your own judgment and your core values. If something doesn't resonate with your purpose, if it doesn't feel like it's going to take you where you need to go? Then you get to say no to it. You are not obligated to settle for less or compromise your vision.

You are not starving. You have shifted out of that season. You are now standing in a season of abundance, and it is your time to feast on the bountiful opportunities that await you. You get to choose the paths that align with your purpose and your gifts, that nourish your soul, and that bring you closer to your dreams.

Don't be afraid to turn away from opportunities that don't serve your higher purpose. Trust in your promise, and have faith that you are destined for greatness. Your feast awaits, and it's time to savor every moment of your abundant journey.

## Time to Write It Out

*In this moment, how will you let your values guide you?*

........................................................................................................

........................................................................................................

........................................................................................................

........................................................................................................

........................................................................................................

........................................................................................................

........................................................................................................

........................................................................................................

........................................................................................................

........................................................................................................

........................................................................................................

........................................................................................................

........................................................................................................

........................................................................................................

........................................................................................................

*Pretty Prayer*

**This is a season of abundance.**

# If the People Around You Don't Believe, Prove Them Wrong

Not everybody's going to believe in you. This is a hard truth that we all have to face.

That lack of belief might come from jealousy. People who don't have the strength or the courage to pursue their own dreams may try to push you down to make themselves feel better about their failures. But sometimes unbelief can come from love, from someone who worries that you'll experience hurt if you fail. They just want to protect you, not realizing that their lack of faith is causing you pain.

Believe me when I say that it happens to everybody. It happened to me. I've faced skepticism and doubt on my path, and I'll tell you, there's only one thing you can do about it: You've got to prove them wrong.

The doubters will always be there with a long list of reasons why they're right, why you're going to fail, why it's too hard, and why you don't have what it takes. You can't talk them into believing in you, because they don't have faith—not like you do.

But that's okay, because you already have all the faith you need—you carry it within yourself. You don't need theirs. And since telling them you have what it takes isn't enough, you just get out there and *do it*. Show them what you're made of. Proving yourself will become your greatest testament to everyone who doubted you along the way.

## Time to Write It Out
*In this moment, how will you have faith in the face of doubt?*

........................................................................................

........................................................................................

........................................................................................

........................................................................................

........................................................................................

........................................................................................

........................................................................................

........................................................................................

........................................................................................

........................................................................................

........................................................................................

........................................................................................

........................................................................................

........................................................................................

*Pretty Prayer*

**You've got all the faith you need.**

# Stop Overthinking

You start to plan. You weigh the pros and cons of a situation. You try to figure out the best strategy, see if you can figure out all the angles. Which is the right move? Maybe the best thing to do is wait and see. But if you wait too long, you might miss your shot.

Overthinking is a hater. It comes in disguise, blending in with strategizing. But it's an unwelcome shadow that constantly whispers doubts and questions into our minds, clouding our judgment and paralyzing us. It can escalate into a relentless cycle of second-guessing, worrying about the past, and fearing the future.

Thinking is one thing. You want to be thoughtful about your choices—but *overthinking* rarely leads to better decisions. Instead, it robs you of your peace, wastes precious time and energy, and breeds unnecessary anxiety. Overthinking is like getting caught in quicksand. The more you struggle with it, the deeper you sink, making it harder to break free. It drains your energy, clouds your judgment, and leaves you feeling stuck.

So how do you get out?

First, you gotta recognize that it's a habit, which means it's something you can change. You have control over it. Practice mindfulness and awareness—notice when you're starting to overthink something, and focus on what you can control *right now* instead of getting lost in the what-ifs and hypotheticals. Challenge your negative thinking, and remind yourself of your strengths—and then go for it! Don't stay stuck! If it doesn't work out, that's okay; at least you *did something*. You pulled yourself out of the quicksand, and that's what's going to keep you moving forward on your path.

## Time to Write It Out

*In this moment, how will you challenge yourself to stop overthinking?*

...................................................................................................

...................................................................................................

...................................................................................................

...................................................................................................

...................................................................................................

...................................................................................................

...................................................................................................

...................................................................................................

...................................................................................................

...................................................................................................

...................................................................................................

...................................................................................................

*Pretty Prayer*

**Make sure you're thinking . . . not overthinking.**

# I'm Not Rushing God's Timing

God has it all figured out. He knows when everything will align for you, because He can see all the different patterns and how everything in this world will come together and split apart.

If it feels like it's all going too slow, like nothing is happening even though you're working so hard all the time—you've got to trust God's timing.

I remember when I first turned up on social media, doing all my skits and trying out all my characters. I was pouring my heart and soul into it, and it seemed like nothing ever paid off. And I got frustrated and felt like I was doing it all for nothing—but of course that wasn't true. I was just the new actress on the block, and I had to go through my process. I had to hone those characters and perfect my timing. I had to get funnier. God knew all that, so He gave me the time and space I needed to sharpen my skills. He allowed me to move through my process so I could get to my promise. Looking back, I can see how every setback, every delay, was actually a divine opportunity for growth and development. God was using those moments to mold me into the person I needed to be, to prepare me for the blessings that were yet to come.

So if you feel like everything is moving too slowly, take

heart and trust in God's plan for your life. He is always working behind the scenes, orchestrating the perfect sequence of events to bring your dreams to fruition. Keep pushing forward, keep honing your skills, and above all, keep trusting in the wisdom of God's timing. For when the moment is right, all the pieces will fall into place, and you'll find yourself exactly where you're meant to be.

## Time to Write It Out
*In this moment, how will you trust in God and keep moving forward?*

........................................................................................

........................................................................................

........................................................................................

........................................................................................

........................................................................................

........................................................................................

........................................................................................

........................................................................................

........................................................................................

........................................................................................

*Pretty Prayer*

**God's timing is always perfect.**

# If You Can Look Up, You Can Get Up

L ife has a funny way of throwing unexpected challenges our way, sometimes knocking us off our feet when we least expect it. We'll be going about our day, thinking everything is going great, and then *bam!*— we're on our backs wondering what the heck happened.

And yeah, it's painful! We bang our knees and scrape our palms, and sometimes we need a moment to let it out—because it hurts, and it's okay to be upset. It's okay to feel bruised and battered, both physically and emotionally. You might feel defeated and discouraged. You might even be tempted to stay down, wallowing in self-pity. But you don't get to do that, because that is *not* where your journey ends.

When you're knocked down, don't just hang your head. When you're face-to-face with the cold, hard ground, you've got to remember that falling is not failing. It's just a single stumble on your path to success. Look up. Look at the open space above you, the vast expanse of possibilities stretching outward. Look for the helping hands reaching down to lift you up again.

Because here's your Pretty Truth: *As long as you have the strength to look up, you have the strength to get up.* You have the power to shake off the dust, wipe away the tears, and stand tall once more. With each fall and with each subsequent rise, you become stronger, wiser, and more resilient.

## Time to Write It Out
*In this moment, how will you look up?*

........................................................................................
........................................................................................
........................................................................................
........................................................................................
........................................................................................
........................................................................................
........................................................................................
........................................................................................
........................................................................................
........................................................................................
........................................................................................
........................................................................................
........................................................................................
........................................................................................

*Pretty Prayer*

**It's not about how many times we fall. It's about how many times we rise again.**

# DAY THIRTY-EIGHT

## Posture Your Heart to Love Again

I'm going to tell you a little bit of my business. I don't normally do this, because I don't know who's reading this. I don't know your name. But if you're called to this book, then you're called to me. So let's get to it.

I was in a relationship for five years, and it was so hard. It was confusing and hurtful, a draining roller coaster of denials and hurt. And when I finally got out of it, I didn't know whom to trust or even how to trust at all. I thought I would never love or date again, because how could I give anyone a chance when I was so broken?

It was a long time before God sent me peace. It didn't come in the form of another human being, from falling in love again or anything like that—it was *internal* peace. I realized that I didn't have to let myself be walked all over, connived, or manipulated—I was free, able to grow, elevate, love, and see myself as an empowered woman.

And yeah, years later a guy came around and swept me off my feet. I opened my heart to him, and I loved it . . . but after a while, I realized it wasn't right, and I began feeling echoes of my past relationship. He started to get on my nerves, so he had to go. And it was fine—it didn't hurt me like it had before, because I had love for myself. I had love within me, for me. And whenever the next person comes around, I know that I love myself enough that he's not gonna play with me. My discernment is heightened, and if a brother comes my way, he's gotta come correct.

I learned how to posture my heart to love—not for another person but for me. Anybody that comes into your life, do not let them play with you. Do the internal work before you try loving somebody else again, because if you don't, you'll always attract somebody who isn't worthy of you. You have to love *you*, first and foremost.

## Time to Write It Out
*In this moment, how will you allow love for yourself into your heart?*

....................................................................................................

....................................................................................................

....................................................................................................

....................................................................................................

....................................................................................................

....................................................................................................

....................................................................................................

....................................................................................................

*Pretty Prayer*

**Are you doing the internal work to love again?**

# DAY THIRTY-NINE

## Your Dreams Don't Have to Make Sense to Others

Sometimes people just aren't going to get what you're about.

My dad loved me and thought I was talented, but he didn't want me to pursue my dreams. It's not that he thought they were bad; he just didn't get it. He didn't see that there would be any money in it. His concerns were rooted in practicality—in his eyes, pursuing my dreams seemed like a risky gamble, and I was likely to end up disappointed and with no way to support myself.

That was okay—I went after what I wanted anyway. Yeah, I know, I'm hardheaded, but that's me. I understood that my dreams were not contingent on external validation. I didn't need his approval or anyone else's—I believed in myself, and that was enough. I made the choice to honor my truth and to follow the path that resonated with my soul. My dreams were mine and mine alone to pursue.

You don't have to prove anything to anybody else. Your dreams are *yours*. You're the only one who knows what's right for you. You know what your gifts are, and it's up to you to decide what to do with them. You are the author of your own destiny. You don't need outside validation, but just in case you want it anyway, here you go: *I believe in you.*

Your dreams are valid, and you are worthy of pursuing them wholeheartedly. Never allow the doubts or misgivings of others to dim your faith in yourself.

## Time to Write It Out

*In this moment, how will you keep dreaming even when somebody tells you to stop?*

........................................................................................................

........................................................................................................

........................................................................................................

........................................................................................................

........................................................................................................

........................................................................................................

........................................................................................................

........................................................................................................

........................................................................................................

........................................................................................................

........................................................................................................

........................................................................................................

........................................................................................................

*Pretty Prayer*

**Just do you and be you!**

## DAY FORTY

# Your Difference Is Your Power

D on't you dare try to be like everybody else.

I know it's tempting. You see a person's success, and you think, *Okay, that's how it's done.* Or worse, people might tell you that you have to be like somebody else—that's definitely happened to me, when someone in charge told me that I was being "too much" or that I needed to be more like so-and-so.

But they were wrong, because it's only by being *me* that I've found my success.

You're not going to get anywhere trying to be somebody else. You'll just be a pale imitation of whatever they're doing—and who wants to live their life like that?

You've got your own gifts to share! God gave them to *you,* not to anybody else, and if you go around keeping them under wraps and pretending to be like all the other people, then they're just going to go to waste. There's only one *you* in this world, and that is your greatest asset. Your individuality is what holds the key to your success. Embracing your gifts means embracing your passions, your authenticity, and your individuality—all the things that make you unique. It means trusting your intuition and forging your own path, even when it diverges from the beaten track.

Yes, it might be easier to blend in, to follow the crowd, to play it safe. But where's the fun in that? Embrace your uniqueness, celebrate your individuality, and trust that your path to success lies in being unapologetically you. Because it's when you dare to stand out that you truly shine.

## Time to Write It Out

*In this moment, how will you stay true to what makes you unique?*

_Pretty Prayer_

**Your weirdness is your creativity.**

# Victorious Friends

## What Makes You Victorious?

*Victorious to me is happiness. I don't care about winning anything against anybody. I care about being happy. If what I'm doing is making me happy, if I wake up every day and everyone I love is happy and goes to bed happy—then that is victory.*

> CHARLAMAGNE THA GOD, radio and television personality, author, and co-host of the nationally syndicated radio show *The Breakfast Club*

*What makes me victorious? God, for one. He gave me resilience, tenacity—oh, and empathy too. I'm a fighter, but I'm nice about it. LOL!*

> TISHA CAMPBELL, actress, singer, playwright, producer, and philanthropist

*God.*

> CHANCE THE RAPPER, three-time Grammy Award–winning rap artist, songwriter, producer, and philanthropist

*What makes me victorious is that I always move with pure intentions no matter the circumstance, and there is victory in that. Because there is victory in knowing that I did right by God and other people at all times.*

PINKY COLE, creator of the renowned
restaurant chain Slutty Vegan

*I find victory in being willing to step out of my comfort zone and embrace new challenges.*

*My courage. I'm not scared of anything. I was on top of a damn plane over the ocean. Fear doesn't live in me.*

BLAMEITONKWAY, social media star, award-winning comedian,
TV personality, actor, producer, and business mogul

*Being connected to the Source makes me victorious! This actors' strike made me realize my job is not my source, my money is not my source, my title is not my source. All the things that are of the world [are] "here today, gone today!" I lost everything because I was connected to the physical things of the world. Money comes and goes; jobs and titles come and go. God is the source! He'll never leave nor forsake me. I started focusing on the things in the spirit, and now, because I am connected to the Source, I'll always be victorious!*

TA'RHONDA JONES, actress, producer,
philanthropist, and rapper

*The Fight.*

BRETT BERISH, CEO of Sovereign Brands

# You're So Busy in the Fight You Lose Sight of the Victory

Get ready, because I've got a Pretty Truth: *You're never going to get to your final Pretty Victory.*

Does that sound harsh? It's not. It's a gift, because here's what it means: *There is no final victory.* You're never going to be finished winning. There will always be another success, another dream made real, because you'll never stop growing, creating, and thriving. You're going to have victory after victory your whole life long. You will never reach a summit with no more peaks to conquer; your potential is boundless, and your capacity for success is infinite.

We're over forty days into our hundred days, and you've probably been winning for a while now. You probably didn't even pause to celebrate them, though—just checked them off your to-do list and moved on to the next task, the next part of the fight.

You deserve better than that! Baby, you deserve to bask in your victories, flex a little and take pride in all that you have accomplished. If you don't pause and take the time to celebrate, you'll get lost in the endless battle, never realizing how much you've already won. You'll lose sight of how strong you are and the resilience that has brought you so far already. It's time to celebrate your Pretty Victories, both past and present, with boundless gratitude, knowing that there is always more to come.

## Time to Write It Out

*In this moment, how will you celebrate your Pretty Victories?*

_Pretty Prayer_

**You're never gonna be done winning.**

# God's Not Gonna Let You Stay Complacent

In 2016 I got fired from my job at a record label.

At the time, I was very upset about it. I didn't know what I was going to do for money, plus I had all these friends and people I loved at that job, and I was worried we were going to grow apart. Although I did lose that job, I won something else in the end. I received the gift of clear sight, the knowledge that more was available to me than this job that really wasn't going anywhere. The bonds that were holding me back were cut, and I was free to soar high.

Even when I was still at the job and loving it and working hard, I knew it wasn't what I was meant to do. I was okay with that, because I figured it was still fun. And I could work on myself and my skits in my spare time, right?

Wrong. That wasn't enough, and God knew that. I had gotten complacent, and God wasn't going to stand for that. He pushed me to my divine purpose and into my next season, and I wouldn't be where I am today if I *hadn't* gotten fired.

Now, was I happy about it at the time? Hell no!

But listen up—getting fired is not that bad, people! You are just getting pushed into your next season. Things that seem bad can actually work for your greater good, and these are just the moments when you have to lean in and trust God's plan. So don't give up, and don't get too comfortable in that nine-to-five.

## Time to Write It Out

*In this moment, how will you prepare yourself for your next season?*

........................................................................................
........................................................................................
........................................................................................
........................................................................................
........................................................................................
........................................................................................
........................................................................................
........................................................................................
........................................................................................
........................................................................................
........................................................................................
........................................................................................
........................................................................................

*Pretty Prayer*

**Don't get too comfortable sitting at that front desk.
Go be your own boss.**

# DAY FORTY-THREE

# For the Women: Is It
# Your Beauty Alone?

I was raised on a steady diet of compliments from my mama, who made sure I knew I was beautiful inside and out. To make sure I knew I was that girl, she'd hype me up—talking about how cute my freckles were and telling me I had a great figure, such a gorgeous face, all of that—so that when I went out in the world, I walked with my head held high.

And when I got into the entertainment industry, I thought, *I'm so pretty that it's going to get me everything I want.*

I was wrong.

Pretty ain't gonna get you in the door, baby! Being the hardest worker in the room and standing on your business—that's what's going to get you in the door.

Thank God I was told I was beautiful, because it gave me confidence. But I was also told I was smart, daring, courageous, and full of life—and *those* qualities are what I really needed to hold close to my heart to succeed. I carried all of them with me so that nobody could tell me I was just a pretty face.

Your worth lies not in how you look but in who you are and in what you bring to the table. Beauty is a gift, but it's not your defining feature. You are so much more than that. Beauty alone ain't gonna get you far. Never forget the strength of your mind, the depth of your character, and the power of your spirit.

## Time to Write It Out
*In this moment, how will you celebrate your inner beauty?*

........................................................................................................

........................................................................................................

........................................................................................................

........................................................................................................

........................................................................................................

........................................................................................................

........................................................................................................

........................................................................................................

........................................................................................................

........................................................................................................

........................................................................................................

........................................................................................................

........................................................................................................

........................................................................................................

*Pretty Prayer*

**Sis, bring more to the table than just your looks.**

# DAY FORTY-FOUR

# Who Are You, King?

I have so many guy friends, and I call them kings. But I want to know—who are they?

King, whoever you are, whoever is reading this, who are you? How are you feeling? What is today like for you?

Because nobody ever asks a Black man, "How are you feeling?"

Nobody inquires about the emotional landscape of the Black male experience, as if society has decided that our kings don't get to have emotions, that they don't get to have trauma—when they have faced so much and done so much for us all.

I want to be the girl in the room who makes someone feel whole and appreciated—because nobody ever gave a Black man flowers. Nobody ever gave a Black man a hand and said, "You're okay." Nobody ever asked, "What is your identity? What is your trauma? What have you faced?"

I know who you are, King.

You are worthy. You are special. You are awesome. You are a leader. You are an alpha. You are seen. You will get everything your heart desires. You are the architect of your destiny and the guardian of your dreams. Your identity is a mosaic of triumphs and trials, victories and vulnerabilities, and it is through embracing every facet of your being that you will emerge victorious. Stand tall in your power.

## Time to Write It Out
*In this moment, how can you be true to your full self?*

........................................................................................

........................................................................................

........................................................................................

........................................................................................

........................................................................................

........................................................................................

........................................................................................

........................................................................................

........................................................................................

........................................................................................

........................................................................................

........................................................................................

........................................................................................

........................................................................................

........................................................................................

*Pretty Prayer*

**Here are your flowers, my kings.**

# DAY FORTY-FIVE

# The Power of Positivity

We've talked about how you have to get out of that negativity—clear out those what-ifs and let go of all that doubt. But once you've done that, you gotta put something else in that space. You gotta replace those fears with confidence, exchange self-doubt for self-belief, and put some positivity in place of all that negativity.

And you're gonna have to do that even when things aren't going so great. Positivity doesn't just mean hoping everything is going to work out. It means choosing to see the good in every situation—including when everything seems to go wrong. Positivity means trusting in God's plan for you and looking at every L not as a loss but as a lesson.

When you're faced with a challenging situation, shift your perspective. Instead of focusing on what's going wrong, pay attention to what's going right. What can you learn from this experience? How can it help you grow? If you look hard enough, you can find the good in every situation. Of course, you won't be able to do that if everyone around you is complaining all the time, bringing all that negative energy into your life. You're going to need to surround yourself with positive, uplifting people who will support and encourage you and who are working to see the good in their own lives. Because positivity is contagious, and that's the kind of flu you wanna catch.

Positivity is a choice you make every day to see the good, to be grateful, and to transform your mind, your heart, and your life.

## Time to Write It Out
*In this moment, how will you spread positivity?*

.................................................................................................
.................................................................................................
.................................................................................................
.................................................................................................
.................................................................................................
.................................................................................................
.................................................................................................
.................................................................................................
.................................................................................................
.................................................................................................
.................................................................................................
.................................................................................................
.................................................................................................

*Pretty Prayer*

**There is good in every situation. Look for it.**

# DAY FORTY-SIX

# Get *Out* of Your *Head*!

Okay, so get out of your head. No, really—get out of your head. Get *out* of your *head*! Lord, get out of your head.

I know everybody keeps saying to stop worrying, stop overthinking—and trust me, I know it's not that easy. I know that your brain isn't like a light switch; you can't just turn it on or off whenever you want to. Sometimes you're up all night because your brain is spinning through thoughts you don't want to have—intrusive thoughts telling you that you're not good enough, that you're going to fail, that somebody else is better than you—and rehearsing all your mistakes and your worst moments.

I've been there. I had my first overthinking moment after college, and I didn't know what the hell I was going through. At that point, I felt lost in the forest of my mind; what was once a space of growth and clarity became fogged with spiraling thoughts.

But I'm here to tell you right now—you don't have to stay in that. You can climb out. You can prosper and get everything your heart desires if you believe in yourself and your purpose and you trust in your process. The enemy will lie to you. He will tell you all sorts of things, get into your head to try to convince you that you're not good enough. He'll make you feel like you don't even want to try—like you don't even want to get out of bed in the morning. But there is a higher power, and He will lead you out of those dark places. You do not have to stay in that place of darkness, of feeling alone. Your victory awaits you at the end of these pages.

## Time to Write It Out

*In this moment, how will you speak louder than your intrusive thoughts?*

......................................................................................................
......................................................................................................
......................................................................................................
......................................................................................................
......................................................................................................
......................................................................................................
......................................................................................................
......................................................................................................
......................................................................................................
......................................................................................................
......................................................................................................

*Pretty Prayer*

**Get out of your big head. That's it and that's all.**

# DAY FORTY-SEVEN

## Stop Failing You

It's easy to get in the habit of blaming everybody else for what's going wrong in our lives—but the truth is, we have no one to blame but ourselves.

When something goes wrong, you have to look in the mirror. Who's failing? Not your mom or your daddy, not your principal or your manager or your business partner. It's you. You have to start the engine of your life and take control.

Your victory is in *your* hands, nobody else's. We give too much to other people when we ask, "What should I do? Do you think I should go for this? Tell me what you would do." Only you know what you want and what is right for you. When you ask somebody for advice and you follow it and it doesn't work out, it's not their fault—it's *yours*. You lost sight of you, and you didn't believe in you. Don't start looking around for someone to blame, because it's not anybody else's fault that you didn't shoot your shot! You didn't set yourself up, wake yourself up, push yourself to your highest potential.

Maybe you're procrastinating on your greatness. Maybe you've gotten too comfortable. Maybe you feel like you're being surpassed by other people; maybe you've dropped the ball, or you feel like somebody else did.

Don't worry about any of them—their failures aren't your problem. Focus on *you*, on your purpose and your goals. When you do that, everything else will fall into place.

## Time to Write It Out

*In this moment, how will you recognize when you're failing yourself?*

_____

_____

_____

_____

_____

_____

_____

_____

_____

_____

_____

_____

_____

_Pretty Prayer_

**Stop blaming everyone else for your failures.**

# DAY FORTY-EIGHT

## The Spirit of the Servant

I want you to ask yourself, *Who does God want me to be in this season?*

We spend so much of our lives shaping ourselves to be a certain way for others. As a kid, I pasted a smile on my face because I thought that would make everyone around me happy—but I wanted my mom and dad to see beyond my smiles, to recognize when I was hurting, wasn't feeling good, or was fearful of something. And because they loved me, they could see what was really going on, just like you notice when your friend is not being their true self, when they're hiding behind their smile.

But what is that smile in service of? Who are we smiling *for*? It's not for the people we love or who truly love us—because they want us to be who we really are in all our complex emotions, the happiness and the sadness, the joy and the pain, and everything in between. They want it all, unfiltered and unapologetic. And why shouldn't we give it to them? Why shouldn't we give our true selves?

Who are you, truly? Who do you really want to be? I can see beyond your smile. I can see the brave, powerful person who feels so much more than a bland, soulless picture smile. The world deserves to see you in all your fullness—

and you deserve to live as your true self. You aren't meant to be a servant of quiet smiles. You are here to speak your truth, to live boldly, and to radiate your unique brilliance. You are a masterpiece in progress, continuously evolving and growing into the person you were always meant to be. Don't hide behind that smile—let your light shine brightly, and the world will be a better place because you're in it.

## Time to Write It Out
*In this moment, who do you want to be in the world?*

........................................................................................................

........................................................................................................

........................................................................................................

........................................................................................................

........................................................................................................

........................................................................................................

........................................................................................................

........................................................................................................

........................................................................................................

........................................................................................................

........................................................................................................

*Pretty Prayer*

**Smile for yourself and yourself alone.**

# Change Your Mess into a Message

We have a habit of blaming ourselves for our mistakes. It's almost like we *want* to feel guilty about them so we can linger in our faults, mess, trauma, anxiety, and depression. Not today, friend! It's not happening on my watch! It may be hard to get out of that space because it feels familiar, and you might feel like if you stay in your mess and don't try again, nothing can go wrong because everything already has.

Don't let that happen. Don't let your mess convince you that you're not worth the effort to make moves and push forward. You've been there before, and I know you don't want that to happen again. You can't move in mess. You can't sleep or accomplish anything. You just sit there. And listen—it's okay to sit in the mess for a little while. I'm human; I do that. But I don't lie in it. I don't sit there for hours that turn into days, weeks, months, and years. That's time wasted, accomplishments on hold, and your brain getting fogged up.

Here's a Pretty Truth: *Change your mess into a message.* What brings you happiness, joy, satisfaction? What heals you and makes you whole? If you start feeling caught up in self-blame for any mistakes you made (and remember, we *all* make mistakes; they're going to happen, and you gotta just move on), you know you need to stop yourself in your tracks right now, before you get stuck again. Get up from where you are and make a change. Change your environment; change a friend. Go to a secret place and pray. Find something that feels good. Get up and go soar high.

## Time to Write It Out

*In this moment, how will you get up from where you are and make a change?*

...................................................................................................................
...................................................................................................................
...................................................................................................................
...................................................................................................................
...................................................................................................................
...................................................................................................................
...................................................................................................................
...................................................................................................................
...................................................................................................................
...................................................................................................................

*Pretty Prayer*

**Turn your mess into a message.**

# DAY FIFTY

## Celebrate!

You're halfway through! You made it! Today, you gotta celebrate all the progress you've made and take a moment to recognize how much you've already accomplished.

Look back on the goals you set for yourself. Have you been making progress? Even if you're not yet where you want to be, you still have to pat yourself on the back for all the steps you took on your journey. Maybe you've become more confident, more resilient, more self-reliant. These internal changes matter just as much as anything that's happening on the outside—maybe even more. Every step forward is a victory.

So go treat yourself, because you deserve it. It doesn't have to be anything big—maybe just go get some ice cream, go home early, or go out with your friends. And don't keep your achievements to yourself! Celebrate with someone you trust who cares about you and supports you. Let their encouragement lift you up and inspire you to keep going.

I am so proud of you. Walk tall in your pride in yourself so you can look back at how far you've come. Keep up the amazing work, stay focused, and continue to believe in yourself. The best is yet to come.

# Time to Write It Out

*In this moment, reflect on what has changed
for you in the past fifty days.*

........................................................................................

........................................................................................

........................................................................................

........................................................................................

........................................................................................

........................................................................................

........................................................................................

........................................................................................

........................................................................................

........................................................................................

........................................................................................

........................................................................................

........................................................................................

........................................................................................

........................................................................................

........................................................................................

........................................................................................

*Pretty Prayer*

**You're halfway, baby! Keep going!**

# *Pretty Victory*

## *Word Search*

### *Time for Some Fun!*

| A | P | R | O | C | E | S | S | Y | W | J | R | E | T | H | G | U | A | L | S |
|---|---|---|---|---|---|---|---|---|---|---|---|---|---|---|---|---|---|---|---|
| L | U | U | B | V | E | S | N | W | H | T | I | A | F | A | V | I | S | G | J |
| B | F | R | Z | B | C | L | Y | C | G | O | Y | V | E | E | W | P | S | B | I |
| K | G | G | M | W | A | K | S | N | E | B | P | S | L | O | V | E | E | W | Y |
| N | H | G | I | G | R | M | D | I | B | A | O | Z | Y | T | O | E | N | A | T |
| R | G | D | C | N | G | I | M | Q | S | P | P | E | A | C | E | T | E | B | I |
| M | Z | M | H | I | J | H | Y | S | R | G | V | O | X | P | N | O | V | I | V |
| G | B | U | U | L | O | B | B | U | O | M | N | W | C | R | B | X | I | U | I |
| K | F | O | W | A | R | X | P | R | L | R | Q | I | K | F | P | O | G | Q | T |
| P | N | D | E | E | O | C | T | P | V | P | D | X | S | D | R | K | R | P | A |
| J | O | A | C | H | Y | R | O | T | C | I | V | R | E | S | Z | V | O | R | E |
| M | P | N | R | P | E | T | K | K | Y | O | R | T | E | P | E | M | F | J | R |
| B | T | A | A | Z | S | N | K | S | Z | O | N | P | N | A | R | L | H | H | C |
| R | F | G | V | M | B | B | Z | X | F | E | E | P | R | O | M | E | B | Z | R |
| G | I | T | U | Y | M | N | S | O | L | G | R | S | U | O | U | P | T | W | T |
| L | G | V | S | Q | I | M | Y | A | A | A | Q | A | A | A | M | V | H | T | G |
| X | S | T | A | R | T | G | T | L | Y | H | Y | W | G | E | O | I | K | I | Y |
| T | E | O | Z | C | P | Z | N | E | K | R | T | H | L | M | L | D | S | Y | S |
| H | T | D | E | U | N | V | R | M | G | W | S | L | O | D | W | E | W | E | N |
| S | U | C | C | E | S | S | Z | Y | P | O | Q | S | L | L | O | E | R | F | U |

| | | | | |
|---|---|---|---|---|
| PRETTY | LOVE | PROCESS | HEALING | SUCCESS |
| VICTORY | PURPOSE | GIFT | LAUGHTER | DREAM |
| STAR | BLESSINGS | PRAYER | GRACE | TALENTED |
| PEACE | RELEASE | FORGIVENESS | FAITH | |
| | PROMISE | | CREATIVITY | |

# *Pretty Challenge*

## *List Your Support System*

### *Whom Can You Call On for Help?*
### *Who Are Your Angels?*

# DAY FIFTY-ONE

## Sir, What's on Your Mind?

As a child, I was always so curious about my daddy. I wanted to know so much about what he was thinking and feeling. With Caribbean parents, you never know what they're thinking—and it's even worse with men. You could see it in their faces and mannerisms and try to guess, but you could never *really* know.

Nobody asks a man what's on his mind. He's supposed to be so strong (and he *is* so strong, make no mistake about that) so we just pass him by, assuming he's doing just fine. Nobody digs down deep, past the social niceties of "How you doin' today?" "Oh, I'm fine, pretty good, can't complain." No, what's *really* on your mind? How are you feeling? Since nobody takes the time to listen, all that men hear are the voices of their traumas and fears, and they can't calm them down . . . which makes those fears fester and come out in anger, defensiveness, and toxic masculinity.

So I want to take the time to ask—King, have you fed your spirit? Have you fed your body? What have you done to cope with what you've been through as a child? Where's your shoulder to lean on?

# Time to Write It Out

*In this moment, write it down—what's really on your mind?*
*For the ladies, write down how you will ask the men in your*
*life this question. How will you show up for them?*

........................................................................................................

........................................................................................................

........................................................................................................

........................................................................................................

........................................................................................................

........................................................................................................

........................................................................................................

........................................................................................................

........................................................................................................

........................................................................................................

........................................................................................................

........................................................................................................

........................................................................................................

........................................................................................................

........................................................................................................

*Pretty Prayer*

**God will give you a sound mind through it all.**
**Trust you; trust Him.**

# DAY FIFTY-TWO

## Trust *You*

We are always asking everybody else for their opinions, calling up our friends, our cousins, our aunties, saying, "What do you think about this relationship? What do you think about this opportunity? Does this skit work? How do I look? Am I doing the right thing?" And while we're waiting for their answers, we are forgetting that the answer is in God's will—and it's up to us to lean on Him for guidance.

Nobody's going to take you to the next level but you. No one's going to put in the work but you. It's important to get feedback and encouragement and support—but *you* are the one with your gift, and only you can use it. God gave it to *you*, and it's your responsibility to honor that gift by staying true to your own values and instincts. You are the one with intimate knowledge of your dreams and how to make them come true. Your wisdom is waiting for you to listen.

So stop asking everybody for their opinions, because let's be real—they're probably going to be wrong. You know what's true and right for you on your path. You know what sounds good for you. You know what looks good for you. You know the right thing to do *for you*. Stop looking to the left and to the right. Look inside, to the center of yourself—because that's where God's guidance is going to come from. It's only when you honor your own truth that you can fully step into your purpose and unleash your purpose on the world.

## Time to Write It Out
*In this moment, how will you rely on yourself?*

........................................................................

........................................................................

........................................................................

........................................................................

........................................................................

........................................................................

........................................................................

........................................................................

........................................................................

........................................................................

........................................................................

........................................................................

*Pretty Prayer*

**You're the one who will have to take the risks.
You're the one with the faith.**

# Work with What You Already Have

When I was feeling depressed and stuck, uncertain about what I was supposed to do or how to move forward, I would pray to God, saying, "Please, God, I need you to show me what I need to do. Give me something; show me the way."

And God would say to me, "You already have a gift in your hand. Refresh it. Renew it. Restart it."

Sometimes I think God must want to throw His hands up and say, "What are you all doing down there?" We're here praying for Him to please show us the way, give us clarity, give us whatever our heart desires, and He's like, "I already gave you a gift! What are you doing with it?"

We all have our own unique and precious gifts, bestowed on each of us by God with love and divine grace. Maybe you've got a gift of building businesses, playing football, singing, or making art—whatever it is, *it is there within you*. And if you're not feeling it, you've got to speak with yourself, remind yourself that it's there. You just have to refresh it, elevate it, and *use it*.

You have a gift in your hands—so don't always be asking God for guidance or questioning your gift when it's already in you. It is not something to passively receive and then forget. And it's not for God to bless you with your gift over and over again—it is a one-time thing! Your gift is a treasure that has been entrusted into your care, and it's up to you to renew it and restart it and *work on it*!

## Time to Write It Out
*In this moment, how will you refresh and renew your gift?*

.................................................................................................
.................................................................................................
.................................................................................................
.................................................................................................
.................................................................................................
.................................................................................................
.................................................................................................
.................................................................................................
.................................................................................................
.................................................................................................
.................................................................................................
.................................................................................................
.................................................................................................

*Pretty Prayer*

**The reason you're losing your edges and having those headaches? You're sleeping on your own potential! Wake up to your blessing!**

# DAY FIFTY-FOUR

# Why Am I Not Happy?

I f you've been blessed and you have a gift from God, then how come you're not happy?

Here's a Pretty Truth: *Nobody's happy all the time. Sometimes life is hard. We struggle at times, and we might get depressed. That's just a part of being human and alive, experiencing all the emotions and all the challenges God has given us to help us grow.*

God didn't put us here to be happy all the time. He didn't give us the gift of happiness—He gave us different gifts and different blessings, like the ability to heal people, make them laugh, or teach them to read or the skills to grow food or create beautiful art. Those blessings are real, and they are within us all.

But happiness? That is for us to choose. Happiness is something we need to seek for ourselves and strive for every single day. We need to decide to find joy in the small, everyday successes, the simple pleasures of a walk in the sunshine or a laugh shared with friends. We need to actively cultivate and tend to our own happiness with acts of kindness, self-care, and gratitude, living in the present moment with an open heart and a caring mind. Happiness is not an end state—you're not going to achieve it like you do with success or victory. You have to decide to feel it in the small moments every day, choosing it the way you choose to love your family, your friends, and yourself.

## Time to Write It Out
*In this moment, how will you choose happiness?*

........................................................................................

........................................................................................

........................................................................................

........................................................................................

........................................................................................

........................................................................................

........................................................................................

........................................................................................

........................................................................................

........................................................................................

........................................................................................

........................................................................................

........................................................................................

........................................................................................

........................................................................................

*Pretty Prayer*

**God gave you the blessing.**
**Happiness is for you to choose.**

# There's Protection in Rejection

When you try for a job you're not qualified for, you might think, *I'm reaching for the stars. I'm striving.* And if they don't hire you, you think it's because you're not good enough.

But there's protection in that rejection. God is saving you from disappointment. That job was the wrong path for you—and if you didn't have the qualifications, that means you didn't do the work you needed to get there. You didn't go through your process before getting to your promise.

Or maybe you got rejected for another reason, like they hired somebody who was even more qualified or who had an inside connection. You might never know why that person got hired and you didn't. But it could be because God saw something bigger for you, something that was a better career path. He was putting you on a different route.

So when you get rejected and catch yourself thinking, *It's me. I'm terrible. I'm never going to amount to anything*—No! You knock that off right now. You were not wrong for that job—that job was wrong for *you*. You didn't need that experience in your spirit, and God was looking out for you. God has something greater in store for you, a divine redirection that will take you toward your true calling, where you can use your gifts to fulfill your purpose. God's not going to let you settle for anything less than that.

## Time to Write It Out

*In this moment, how will you recognize God's hand in the obstacles that come your way?*

........................................................................

........................................................................

........................................................................

........................................................................

........................................................................

........................................................................

........................................................................

........................................................................

........................................................................

........................................................................

........................................................................

........................................................................

........................................................................

........................................................................

*Pretty Prayer*

**God's protection is in the rejection. Just trust Him.**

# DAY FIFTY-SIX

## Don't Overshare

I used to be a talker. As a kid, I got yelled at for telling everybody all my business—I would tell my friends, my family, people I didn't even know, all about everything that was coming up next for me. I thought that everybody would be happy for me. I thought they would want to congratulate me and stand ten toes down with me . . . but that wasn't always the case. Instead, if I told somebody I was going to get a new outfit—guess who'd show up with that outfit before me. Or if I told somebody I was going to try for something, look who would try for the same thing before I even got the chance. My blessings would get delayed because I didn't wait to make sure they were confirmed before I went around telling everybody all about them.

You'd think I'd have learned better by the time I grew up. I'm going around, so excited, telling the people I *thought* were my friends, "MTV got me this new gig! I'm hosting a red carpet! I'm going to be in a movie!" Only, it turned out they weren't my friends at all. They weren't happy for my elevation. They weren't praying for me to rise—deep down, they were praying for my downfall.

There are going to be people like that in your life—people who seem like they're your friends, but in their hearts, they don't want what's best for you. They are struggling with their own envy. You can have generosity in your heart for their pain, but that doesn't mean you have to share your blessings with them. You gotta guard what comes your way so your blessings don't go into the wrong ears and the wrong hearts. Don't overshare.

## Time to Write It Out
*In this moment, how will you protect your blessings?*

........................................................................................................

........................................................................................................

........................................................................................................

........................................................................................................

........................................................................................................

........................................................................................................

........................................................................................................

........................................................................................................

........................................................................................................

........................................................................................................

........................................................................................................

........................................................................................................

*Pretty Prayer*

**Everybody ain't your friend. Period.**

# Jobs Will Come and Go, but Your Calling Won't

You might get fired from a job at some point. You might quit a job that you hate or that isn't leading you forward in your chosen career. And yeah, it's rough, and it feels like a setback. It might seem like you're never going to get ahead or know where your next paycheck is coming from.

But when you have a calling over your life? When you have a gift? Your gift will always have a seat at your table. Your gift will bring you financial freedom.

You cannot shake your gift; you cannot hide it; you cannot kick it to the curb. That calling on your life can be seen a hundred miles away.

And if you dive headfirst into your calling, if you truly commit to it and have faith in it, putting in the hard work and the effort it deserves? Then your gift *will* make you money. Don't keep depending on a job to save you, because you have a gift you need to use. My gift is to make the world laugh—and by doing that, I can turn funny into money. You might think your gift is just something small, nothing that you can live off of—but I'm telling you, God would not do that to you. Your gift is meant to sustain you spiritually, but it's gonna sustain you financially too.

# Time to Write It Out

*In this moment, how will you invest in your gift?*

........................................................................................

........................................................................................

........................................................................................

........................................................................................

........................................................................................

........................................................................................

........................................................................................

........................................................................................

........................................................................................

........................................................................................

........................................................................................

........................................................................................

........................................................................................

........................................................................................

........................................................................................

........................................................................................

........................................................................................

........................................................................................

*Pretty Prayer*

**Who cares if you got fired from that job?**
**Go focus on your calling.**

# Stick to the Program

How are you doing? How's it feeling so far? By now, you've probably got into the rhythm, started seeing some results . . . but you're also probably getting a little tired. You want success to be here already, and you want to take a break.

Don't do it.

You gotta stick with it, all the way through. I know there are distractions. I know you want to be dancing at the club or watching your show or putting your feet up—and trust me, I know you deserve that! You've been working hard. But you gotta keep working hard, because you are worth that hard work.

I bet you've encountered some setbacks. I bet you've hit some obstacles that have shaken your confidence. Did you feel doubt? Did you want to give up?

I'm so proud of you—because you didn't. You're still here. So don't start taking the easy road now. Don't go looking for shortcuts or simple solutions. Stick to the program, and have faith in your own resilience. Trust in the process, and know that what has been promised to you is on its way. You are making it into a reality right now, today, just by reading this and doing the internal work. It is through your dedication to *yourself* and your consistent effort and determination that you will keep moving forward, bringing you closer to your Pretty Victory every single day.

## Time to Write It Out
*In this moment, how will you stay committed to yourself?*

..................................................................................................
..................................................................................................
..................................................................................................
..................................................................................................
..................................................................................................
..................................................................................................
..................................................................................................
..................................................................................................
..................................................................................................
..................................................................................................
..................................................................................................
..................................................................................................
..................................................................................................
..................................................................................................

*Pretty Prayer*

**There aren't any shortcuts to victory.**

# DAY FIFTY-NINE

## Life Be Lifin'

Even in the midst of our trials and tribulations, God is with us. His goodness transcends the setbacks and delays we encounter along life's journey, and no matter what life throws at us, He will still be there, steadfastly guiding us through every storm.

You gotta remember, just because life is lifin' with all its frustrations and challenges doesn't mean God isn't still with you, standing right by your side. He hasn't abandoned you. He's right there, walking alongside you, offering His strength and guidance. All that mess you're going through? That's just *life;* it's just a part of being alive with other humans living out their experience here on this earth. It's not going to be easy all the time. But just because there are challenges doesn't mean you should give up.

*Do not give up.*

Continue to strive for your greatness. Continue to walk in your purpose. Continue to fight.

There is victory at the end of the road, but you have to keep walking it. Even when your legs hurt and your spirit falters, even when you've got blisters and your feet are bloodied—*you have to keep going.* You have a calling with your name on it. You have a gift with your name on it.

You have purpose that only you can fulfill. So just because life is lifin' doesn't mean you can't keep going, because you can. Keep believing in yourself, in your abilities, and in the unwavering presence of God walking alongside you every step of the way.

## Time to Write It Out
*In this moment, how will you keep going when life gets hard?*

.......................................................................................

.......................................................................................

.......................................................................................

.......................................................................................

.......................................................................................

.......................................................................................

.......................................................................................

.......................................................................................

.......................................................................................

.......................................................................................

.......................................................................................

.......................................................................................

*Pretty Prayer*

**There's victory at the end of the tunnel.**

# Breakthrough

We are all waiting on that phone call. You know the one—the call that's your big breakthrough, the opportunity you've been waiting for.

Maybe you've been sitting and waiting for a long time. And in the midst of all that waiting, maybe it's starting to feel like that break is never going to come. Maybe you're watching everybody else have their successes, and you're wondering why it isn't happening for you. Maybe it's starting to feel like no matter what you do, you always end up back at square one, starting over—no matter what you try, it never works out; you never *break through*.

If that's you, here's your Pretty Truth: *It's on its way. You just need to trust the process, trust you, and trust God.*

So stop asking your friends what you should or shouldn't do. Stop asking them for their thoughts on what you're doing wrong and what they're doing right. Stop looking to the left or right, seeing them go by and thinking that means they're surpassing you—because they're not. All it means is that this is their season. Appreciate their season, celebrate with them, understand what it's like, and know that your season will come in its own time. And when it does, you're going to be ready. You're going to know that your season will still have its struggles, its ups and downs, because you'll have watched and supported your friends and learned from them—so when your breakthrough comes, you're gonna *bust out*.

## Time to Write It Out

*In this moment, how will you learn from others so you can be ready when your breakthrough comes?*

........................................................................................

........................................................................................

........................................................................................

........................................................................................

........................................................................................

........................................................................................

........................................................................................

........................................................................................

........................................................................................

........................................................................................

........................................................................................

*Pretty Prayer*

**Stay by your phone. Your breakthrough is one call away.**

# *Victorious Friends*

## *What Makes You Victorious?*

*I'm victorious because I have set up a life and a mindset where I control the outcome of every situation. I know I'll never have control over what other people choose to do or say, but I control what I can stand tall on or choose to walk away from. Whichever I ultimately select, I know that I'm always doing what's best for me and my daughter. That's a victory in my book. I am not a victim in any circumstance. I'm the hero.*

PORSHA WILLIAMS, television and radio personality,
actress, author, and entrepreneur

*Peace and love.*

RICKEY SMILEY, radio and television personality,
comedian, actor, and host of the nationally syndicated,
award-winning program *The Rickey Smiley Morning Show*

*My ability to survive and still be good even when everything else is bad and even when everyone has counted me out.*

REMY MA, Grammy Award–nominated
rapper, actress, and business owner

*I don't let my circumstances stop me. I push through.*

Toya Johnson-Rushing, television personality, businesswoman, and *New York Times* bestselling author

*God.*

Jackie Long, actor, writer, producer, director, and podcast host

*What makes me victorious is knowing that even in my darkest times I am choosing to be resilient. I admit my feelings, and I understand that every day is not gonna be perfect, but I know there is a light at the end of the tunnel. I'm always willing to try again and never give up. Every day we wake up, we have an opportunity to get closer to God and walk in purpose. I choose that every day. Being victorious isn't easy, but it's always worth it. I love you.*

B. Simone, comedian, actress, podcast host, and social media sensation

*Being victorious in your journey as a mother, entrepreneur, and businesswoman means consistently showing up, even when you're worn out. It's about facing overwhelming challenges head-on, persistently pushing through, and demonstrating an unshakable commitment to achieving your dreams and upholding your responsibilities.*

Dr. Rashae Barnes, celebrity publicist and branding expert

# DAY SIXTY-ONE

# Why Are You Doubting Yourself?

Why are you doubting yourself?

Why are you procrastinating on the gift that God gave you? Why do you keep erasing all the successes you have had, all the strength you possess, all the creativity bursting out of you? Why do you keep second-guessing your hopes and dreams?

You're just wasting your time and God's.

Don't you know that when we procrastinate, we delay our own lessons? Don't you know that if we second-guess our own instincts, we lose sight of the path God laid out for us?

When we give in to doubt, we go with plan B instead of plan A—and plan A is the one where you get to live your dream and use the gift God gave you! So stop doubting yourself. No one has the answers but you. No one has the vision but you.

You can do it. I know you're sitting there thinking, *Girl, you don't even know what my dream is. How can you possibly know that?* Believe me, whatever it is, I *know* you can, because that's the kind of faith I have—and it's the kind of faith you need to carry you through the hard times.

It doesn't matter how big your dream is. You can be the

next Michael Jordan. You can be the next Oprah Winfrey. You can be the next Barack Obama. Heck, you can be the next Pretty Vee! You just gotta keep your eyes on it and *keep going.*

## Time to Write It Out
*In this moment, how will you cultivate your faith?*

_____

_____

_____

_____

_____

_____

_____

_____

_____

_____

_____

_____

*Pretty Prayer*

**Stop second-guessing, and just do it!**

# DAY SIXTY-TWO

## Forgiveness

Forgiveness can be a scary thing, and sometimes you're gonna want to push back against it. You might be like "Why am I forgiving them? They hurt me." Or even "Why do I have to say I'm sorry? It happened; it's over." Either way, it's hard. But it's necessary. We've got to put our pride aside. We've got to humble ourselves. We've got to prostrate ourselves. And trust me, it's worth it, because when we forgive and are forgiven? We get so much in return.

At times, I'm like "Why do I have to tell that person sorry? Why do I have to listen to them talk about their issues and problems?" The reason is that it's often all somebody needs to move on with their life, to go to the next steps in their season. Sometimes they just need the person who hurt them to say that they're sorry—it might seem like a small thing, but it can mean so much.

Forgiveness releases trauma on both sides—whether you're the one saying sorry or the one being apologized to. It allows you to let go of all the hurt, all the things you didn't like or understand. Sometimes, all you need is for someone to say, "Hey, do you forgive me?" And other times, all you need is the relief of saying, "Hey, I did the wrong thing. I'm sorry."

We can get so stuck that we can't move forward, either because we're hurt or because we're afraid of admitting we've done wrong. So today, pick up the phone. Call that person who hurt you and say, "Hey, I forgive you." Or ask the one you hurt, "Hey, do you forgive me?"

## Time to Write It Out

*In this moment, how will you do the big, hard thing and move forward with forgiveness?*

......................................................................................................
......................................................................................................
......................................................................................................
......................................................................................................
......................................................................................................
......................................................................................................
......................................................................................................
......................................................................................................
......................................................................................................
......................................................................................................
......................................................................................................
......................................................................................................

*Pretty Prayer*

**Forgive and forget—you are healed.**

# DAY SIXTY-THREE

# Humble Yourself

That small word *humble* can do so much.

I haven't always remembered to stay humble.

I've had my highs, my lows, my in-betweens. There were times I felt like myself and others when I didn't know who I was. And every now and then, God had to put me in a place of stillness because I was feeling myself *too* much!

So I gotta ask you—are you feeling yourself too much? Are you feeling like you've got it all going on? Like you can conquer the world on your own, without leaning on anyone? Are you feeling like you have your own understanding and can move mountains?

Well, I'm here to tell you, you're wrong. Here's a Pretty Truth: *You can't move a mountain. You can't do it all on your own. You don't have it all going on.*

I'm here to tell you to *humble yourself.*

You need God. You need His presence and His guidance. If you don't remember that, successes will be snatched away and opportunities will stay on the horizon because you aren't humble. You can't be bigheaded in your season. If you're trying to tap into any industry—no matter what it is—you have to take direction. You have to always be a student, a great listener. You have to be able to take advice and critiques so you can grow and get to the next level. But if you feel like you know it all, you'll never go anywhere.

Don't you know that you need to humble yourself to get what you need?

## Time to Write It Out

*In this moment, how will you remind yourself to stay humble?*

........................................................................
........................................................................
........................................................................
........................................................................
........................................................................
........................................................................
........................................................................
........................................................................
........................................................................
........................................................................

*Pretty Prayer*

***You! I'm talking to you! Stop being bigheaded, and humble yourself.***

# DAY SIXTY-FOUR

## Talk to Someone

I know the idea of talking to a professional for help sounds crazy. I grew up in a Christian household, and at the time, going to a counselor or therapist was not a thought. The only person who could save me was God.

And that's still true—but God does send vessels to help us in the midst of our discouraging seasons, when our faith can be a little shaky. God sends help when anxiety, nerves, and depression come.

Now, I know you probably talk to your aunties, your pastor, or your friends about things like this, and that's great. But sometimes that's not enough. Because there's only so much a friend or an auntie can do, and there are people who do this for a living, who are trained and called to do this because it's their gift—and they can help you when you need it most. There's no shame in talking to a therapist. Stop being afraid that they might judge you or making the excuse that they don't know you or whatever. Pick up the phone. Do your research, go pray, and then go talk to someone.

Because I promise you, everyone is not out to get you. Not everyone is a bad person. No one is judging you the way you think they are right now. It's okay to talk to someone and share those deep secrets with someone because you can't hold it in anymore—and you don't have to keep holding it in. I promise you, you'll feel worthy and rejuvenated, and you'll find your purpose again. Don't be the person who sits in the sadness, in a dark place. Don't wait until it's too late. Talk to someone.

## Time to Write It Out
*In this moment, how will you open yourself up to someone?*

........................................................................................................
........................................................................................................
........................................................................................................
........................................................................................................
........................................................................................................
........................................................................................................
........................................................................................................
........................................................................................................
........................................................................................................
........................................................................................................

*Pretty Prayer*

**You can't carry your weight alone. Share it with your friend, your counselor, or your pastor, and go get healed. Period.**

# DAY SIXTY-FIVE

## God Will Send Help

I know you feel like you've got to do it alone. I know you think you are walking on your own, with nobody by your side, with no one to help you. But you are never alone—God is always there beside you, and He will always send someone to lift you up when you are down.

Back in 2016, when I wanted to be a radio personality even though I didn't know the first thing about how to make that dream come true, I got so caught up in overthinking, in the what-ifs and the maybes, that I got stuck in a web of negative thoughts. I got depressed. Before that, I didn't even know what depression was, but now I found myself wrapped up in a blanket in my bed, not wanting to get up or get out, not wanting to do anything at all.

And I needed help. I longed for somebody to show me the way, and I asked God to send me help so I could understand what was coming next for me in my season. And you know what? He already had. Because my mom was right there. She prayed for me and with me every day. She helped me rebuild my faith. She opened the door to my bedroom, and she let the devil out—the devil of my own fears and anxieties that had been keeping me stuck there. She opened the door to new possibilities, to a different, broader dream that would make use of my gift in the way that was right for me.

So you know what I want for you? I want you to hold on. Keep going. You *can* overcome your fears, your depression, your anxiety—if you believe you can. And I am here to give you that belief, because I have faith in you. God will send help, if you believe.

## Time to Write It Out
*In this moment, how will you ask for and accept help?*

..................................................................................................
..................................................................................................
..................................................................................................
..................................................................................................
..................................................................................................
..................................................................................................
..................................................................................................
..................................................................................................
..................................................................................................

*Pretty Prayer*

***You never know where your angels are. Your angel could be right in front of your face, if you just believe.***

# DAY SIXTY-SIX

## Smile

When they face rejection or delays or feel overlooked or left out, a lot of people will frown. They let their disappointment show on their faces and allow the whole world to see their hurt and frustration.

But me? I tend to smile.

I smile through the hurt, through the pain, through the rejection. I smile through it all.

I remember how devastated I was when I didn't get picked for *Wild 'N Out* right away—but I kept that smile on my face. I felt like I'd been knocked down, but my posture did not change. I stood up straight and proud, and I walked tall. I never let my pain show.

Why? Because I didn't need everybody around me to know my business. My suffering was my own; I didn't need to perform it for their benefit. But more than that, I knew the pain was temporary. My faith was activated, and I knew that even this setback was simply that—a delay, not a denial.

A delay never means a denial. It is your sign to keep going. The hustle is still on. The goal still has to be reached. Understand that you are called to do great things and that your calling has a purpose. Keep pushing through, and watch how victory comes for you.

So today, change your frown to a smile. Believe that you'll get where you're supposed to be because you have what it takes. It doesn't matter what's happening right now—you *know* it's all going to work out in the end.

## Time to Write It Out
*In this moment, how will you put a smile on your face?*

........................................................................................................................
........................................................................................................................
........................................................................................................................
........................................................................................................................
........................................................................................................................
........................................................................................................................
........................................................................................................................
........................................................................................................................
........................................................................................................................
........................................................................................................................
........................................................................................................................
........................................................................................................................

*Pretty Prayer*

***I'm living my best life.** –Lil Duval*

# Go to God Before You Call Me

Y ou're always asking your friends for advice about what's going on in your life. Why? They are not God. They can't tell you what your life should be. Just like they can't tell you who your baby daddy is sleeping with or whether you should quit your job or not.

Before you pick up your phone to ask your friends about your life or your desires, go to God. He is going to lead you. He will show you in detail what you should do to get to your next season. The only place your friends can take you is to the mall! And you're going to be broke before you get out!

And sometimes—not all the time and not with your true friends—the friends you are asking for advice don't have your best interests at heart. Some of these "friends" want to see you fail; they love to see you miserable, because they want to keep you down low, right beside them. Not sure which kind of friends the people around you are? Go to God first anyway. Then you can call them. If they don't pick up the phone? Great. Don't call them again—let them go. They weren't your true friends, and now you know that.

But even your true friends, who love you and only want the best for you—they don't really know what the best is. Only God knows that! Only God and *you*. So you can call on them for support, but when it comes to knowing what to do? Call on God.

*Pretty Prayer*

**Call on God, not your friends.**

# DAY SIXTY-EIGHT

## Perseverance

I didn't know whether I was going to make it in the entertainment industry. I had faith in myself and my gifts, and I worked hard. But when I hit my setbacks, I didn't know that's all they were—I thought maybe that was the end of the road for me.

Back in 2018, I had an enormous opportunity to get my name in a major retail chain, and I was so excited and proud—but then, out of nowhere, they changed their minds because they didn't like something I'd said on social media. Now, I'm an African American woman. I can say "nigga" if I want to . . . but they didn't agree.

I felt so denied. I felt like I'd failed myself. But I was determined to have my name planted, so I didn't give up. And then a year later I got a call from Citi Trends saying they were going to place my merchandise in over six hundred stores—a bigger and better opportunity. It was like the whole time I was upset about this other thing, God was hard at work on the back end, going, "You can sit in this meeting if you want . . . but I'm lining it up for you over here."

Perseverance means carrying on even when you don't know for sure whether it's going to work out. You can't see the results yet—but you have the belief in yourself that will carry you through. Every challenge you overcome becomes a testament to your courage and makes you strong enough to face the next challenge, and the one after that.

## Time to Write It Out

*In this moment, how will you trust that the results are coming even when you can't see them?*

........................................................................................

........................................................................................

........................................................................................

........................................................................................

........................................................................................

........................................................................................

........................................................................................

........................................................................................

........................................................................................

........................................................................................

........................................................................................

........................................................................................

*Pretty Prayer*

**A setback is nothing but a setup for a comeback!**
**–Willie Jolley**

# Hollywood

Oh Lord, Hollywood. Hol-ly-wood. It can bring you up, but it can also bring you down. Hollywood will love on you, support you, go above and beyond for you—but the minute you say something that Hollywood doesn't like? You're gone. We are living in a cancel-culture world, and that can paralyze you. It can make you want to pretend to be someone you're not, to align yourself with someone else's values and truths—but that is not the road to happiness or to true, meaningful success. If Hollywood is your dream, you gotta know that you have to stay true to *yourself*. You gotta know who you are.

Here's your Pretty Truth: *To make it in this business, you have to be prayed up, keep your faith, and know that you'd better not sell that soul.*

You have to keep God first, through all the uncertainty and adversity—and there will be a lot! You're going to face rejections, so don't get mad when they come. Yeah, I'm talking to you, sis! Come on, boy, don't get mad—it's Hollywood! You gotta know what's for you and what's not. I didn't get every opportunity that came my way. I tried out for movies on Netflix, Starz, and MTV, and when I didn't get them, I thought maybe everybody just saw me as a skit girl with nothing more to offer. But eventually I *did* start landing those roles.

You have to know that when you get denied, you need to keep pushing forward. Don't give up on who you are, and grow that hard skin. Know that God's protection is in those rejections, and start carving out your own niche, creating your own space—one that's true to *you*.

## Time to Write It Out
*In this moment, how will you stay true to yourself in the face of rejection?*

......................................................................................................

......................................................................................................

......................................................................................................

......................................................................................................

......................................................................................................

......................................................................................................

......................................................................................................

......................................................................................................

......................................................................................................

......................................................................................................

*Pretty Prayer*

**Create your own lane so no one can cut you off.**

# Who Are Your Friends?

Friends matter. The company you keep and the conversations you hold matter.

I get so *inspired* by my friends, with all their different personalities and ideas and outlooks—all pushing and going and striving. Whoever is reading this, I think maybe I'm talking to you! I get so inspired by you, because you make me want to work hard to get up to your level. Your energy gives me energy.

I didn't always have friends like that, though. At times, I felt so lazy and depressed, and I just kept sitting back, wondering why I didn't have the drive to push myself . . . Well, it was because the friend beside me had that same low level of energy. I've pushed so many of my friends to do better, and that output of energy drained me so that I didn't have it in me to push myself. And I realized, I gotta find some new friends! These friends ain't pushing me; I'm pushing them—and I'm not getting that help in return.

Who are your friends in this season? Who will have your back? Who will encourage you to be great? I had a whole bunch of friends, and I did not feel inspired. I prayed with them and encouraged them, and all I felt was a drain. I did not feel supported. You have to be in alignment with the people in your life. There has to be a back-and-forth flow of energy so you're both getting fed. Make sure you're surrounding yourself with people who will lift you up.

It's okay to change out your friends. Seasons change, and our friends can change as well. It's okay to let people go. It doesn't mean that you didn't love them or that the friendship wasn't valuable—all it means is that their season of being your friend has passed.

## Time to Write It Out
*In this moment, how will you choose friends that elevate you?*

....................................................................................................

....................................................................................................

....................................................................................................

....................................................................................................

....................................................................................................

....................................................................................................

....................................................................................................

....................................................................................................

*Pretty Prayer*

**Don't be scared to do an Amazon Prime prayer with this one—pray to God to remove the people from your life who don't belong there, and watch . . . They'll be gone overnight.**

# Who Is Supporting You?

I send out devotionals over Instagram every morning, of-fering support to my followers. I don't look for anything in return, but I also ask myself, *Who's going to support me? Who's going to make sure I'm okay?*

At times, I've felt like I didn't have that kind of support, like the energy I gave to others wasn't given to me in return. Whenever the people in my life needed help, I put myself aside for them—but it seemed they weren't willing to do the same for me if I was the one in pain. And I know some of y'all reading this right now feel like you don't have support, like you don't have someone to call on, because you're so busy giving to others and not receiving when it's your turn.

That's a problem; I'm not gonna lie. That tells me you need to get some new friends! But here's something I know for sure: You *do* have support. When I felt that way, like I was giving and not receiving, like nobody was *seeing me* and I was all alone? I wasn't alone at all.

My biggest supporter is my mother. She is one of my best cheerleaders, and in those times I felt like I was down and out, she was right there to pick me back up and say, "I support you in all areas of your life, the highs, the in-betweens, and the lows." And I *know* that you have that too. Someone out there supports you. Someone loves you. Someone wants to encourage you. I'm writing this book because I support you—I want you to get up and get going. You have to reach out to the people who love you, and they will be there for you, always.

## Time to Write It Out

*In this moment, how will you reach out to the people who support and love you?*

........................................................................................
........................................................................................
........................................................................................
........................................................................................
........................................................................................
........................................................................................
........................................................................................
........................................................................................
........................................................................................
........................................................................................
........................................................................................
........................................................................................

*Pretty Prayer*

**You have support, and you are not alone.**
**All you gotta do is reach out.**

# Put the Phone Down

What's the first thing you do when you get up in the morning? Do you pray? Or do you start scrolling through your phone, checking your messages, checking to see what's going on with your friends, what's on social media?

I suggest you put that phone down. It is so important to take a beat in the morning. It is so important to pray, to meditate, to give your hands a rest from that phone. The energy of social media can be so negative, and that can impact your whole day. As soon as you open your phone to that space, your energy shuts down. That can't be the first thing you do to start your day—you want to set yourself up for greatness, create a start to your morning that will carry you through. Social media ain't going nowhere. Your text messages and emails will still be there waiting for you when you're done. Discipline yourself, put that phone down, and get alone with God in a still space.

First thing in the morning, embrace the world. Be present with the moment. You can miss opportunities when you're glued to a screen. We get so distracted by our phones that we're not present in our blessings, and putting those screens down allows us to reclaim time with our family and friends. Know that today's going to be a great day, and step out in the morning to walk in your season of grace.

## Time to Write It Out
*In this moment, how will you set yourself up for greatness in the mornings?*

....................................................................................

....................................................................................

....................................................................................

....................................................................................

....................................................................................

....................................................................................

....................................................................................

....................................................................................

....................................................................................

....................................................................................

....................................................................................

....................................................................................

....................................................................................

*Pretty Prayer*

**I challenge you to pray before you pick up your phone. Can you do it? Ready, set, go—pray.**

# DAY SEVENTY-THREE

## Pain

I f you've been walking alone and in pain for a long time, you might think that's all there is. You almost get used to it and think it's just a normal way of life.

But whoever is reading this—*you don't have to live that way.* You don't have to keep walking and moving with your pain alone. Trust God, trust your path, and understand that there are people who want to help you, who want to see you through your pain. You don't have to carry it alone.

When I was younger, I trusted in my mom and God, and that was it. I didn't think I could rely on anybody else. I had so much pride back then—I never wanted to ask a soul for help. I didn't want anybody to think that I needed them or that they would have one up on me. I didn't want to seem like I was weak or didn't have it all together. But the truth was, I *did* need that help, and I was praying every day for God to send me an angel—when my angels were all around me.

Pride can get in the way of your asking for help. Where is your community? God is sending you help through family, friends, and counselors, and letting them know you need them is not a sign of weakness—it is a sign of strength. Showing that you are vulnerable and want to make changes in your life? That's one of the most powerful things you can do.

You don't have to carry everything alone, and you don't have to take your burdens into your next season. When you're in a space of feeling alone or in pain, reach out to someone. It's okay to let them walk beside you, sharing the weight. It's okay to ask for help.

## Time to Write It Out

*In this moment, how will you put aside your pride and ask for help when you need it?*

........................................................................

........................................................................

........................................................................

........................................................................

........................................................................

........................................................................

........................................................................

........................................................................

........................................................................

........................................................................

*Pretty Prayer*

**Your vulnerability is your superpower.**

# DAY SEVENTY-FOUR

# Stop Being Insecure!

I've got a gift; you've got a gift. It's like God's up there like Oprah, generously handing them out to everybody—we've all got these beautiful, extraordinary, invaluable gifts that the world needs. So why are you out here thinking yours isn't worth it?

You think my gift is any more meaningful than yours is?

Think about your best friend, the way their gift shines through so brightly and you want to do everything you can to encourage them, to push them to share their gift with the world—is *their* gift more meaningful than yours?

Hell no! Every soul on this planet holds a gift that is precious and indispensable. Your gift is like a missing tile in the grand mosaic of humanity, and the world needs it—just as much as it needs any other gift out there that's waiting to be uncovered and discovered. Never doubt the significance of what you bring to the table. It is absolutely worth celebrating and sharing with the world.

Don't you dare be insecure about your talents! They are *yours*, and you should speak out, loud and proud, telling everybody about them—because they deserve to hear it! There are people in this world waiting to hear from you. Are you going to let them down?

# Time to Write It Out

*In this moment, how can you find pride in your gifts?*

........................................................................................

........................................................................................

........................................................................................

........................................................................................

........................................................................................

........................................................................................

........................................................................................

........................................................................................

........................................................................................

........................................................................................

........................................................................................

........................................................................................

........................................................................................

........................................................................................

........................................................................................

........................................................................................

........................................................................................

........................................................................................

*Pretty Prayer*

**Your gift is just as important as anybody else's.**

# Clean Your Hard Drive

When I say "clean your hard drive," I'm not talking about the motherboard on your computer. I'm talking about your mind, your body, your soul—the internal workings of your being. Just like your computer getting a virus, you have unintentionally downloaded so many negative thoughts left over from childhood trauma, divorce, mental illness, or painful memories, and they're all clogging up your hard drive. You gotta clean it out, baby.

You gotta let go of that burden so you can move forward. I see how you keep going back and forth with yourself, but this is your season to get rid of all that garbage, all those viruses, all that evil thinking. You have the power to clean house, to declutter your mind and spirit, and to free yourself from all that's been holding you down. You need to be still and sit with all that you've been through, so that you can finally release it. You need to understand deep within yourself that it's truly in your past and not in your present. It's finished. You get to move on now. This is your moment to break free from that cycle and make space for new, positive energy to flow into your life.

So stop letting the outside noise get into you. Throw up

your walls and protect yourself! You get to choose what you let into your system! Are you going to let the enemy in, or are you going to show him the door? Fortify your defenses and set your boundaries. You have the ultimate say in what you allow into your sacred space.

## Time to Write It Out
*In this moment, how will you clean yourself out?*

........................................................................................................

........................................................................................................

........................................................................................................

........................................................................................................

........................................................................................................

........................................................................................................

........................................................................................................

........................................................................................................

........................................................................................................

........................................................................................................

........................................................................................................

........................................................................................................

........................................................................................................

*Pretty Prayer*

**You have the power to free yourself of your burdens.**

## DAY SEVENTY-SIX

# You Are in Your Birthing Season

Y
ou have been in labor for so long, waiting on this new baby to come, enduring the contractions of life as you strive to bring something new and beautiful into the world. You've had so many setbacks, so many delays and denials, but now it's time for you to birth your gift. This is the last push.

I'm telling you, your time has come. This is your birthing season. This is it—the culmination of all your effort and perseverance. You've been nurturing and growing your gift, but now it's time to labor through the final stages and bring it into the light.

And let me make one thing clear: This message isn't just for the ladies. Fellas, if you're reading this, yes, I'm talking to you too. You're also holding something inside you: your greatness. At this point, you're overdue. Push it out.

The whole world *needs* to see your gift. You keep fighting the contractions, holding it in, staying in the same space—you've been doing that for so long, and it's so painful. It's time to bear down and push past that. Exert every ounce of strength within you to bring forth your brilliance. Don't be afraid to push through the pain, to embrace the discomfort of growth and change. This is your moment to shine, to step into your purpose with confidence and determination. Bring forth that baby, and witness the miracle of your own rebirth.

## Time to Write It Out
*In this moment, how will you push through the final stages?*

........................................................................
........................................................................
........................................................................
........................................................................
........................................................................
........................................................................
........................................................................
........................................................................
........................................................................
........................................................................
........................................................................
........................................................................
........................................................................

*Pretty Prayer*

**Push your gift forward!**

# DAY SEVENTY-SEVEN

# I Will Never Dumb Down My Life to Please a Soul

I fought hard to reach the point where I stand today. I've invested unwavering effort and determination into securing my success. And I promise you, I am not going to pretend that I am not successful. Why would I do that?

Yet it seems like people want us to, doesn't it? As if we're supposed to downsize our own achievements, saying, "Oh no, it's no big deal"—when it *is* a big deal. We're supposed to deny ourselves and our accomplishments so we don't seem like we're bigheaded or something? Now, don't get me wrong; I'm not saying you've got to go around bragging or talking yourself up like you're more than you are yet—nobody likes that. Overhyping yourself doesn't make you seem big; it makes you seem small. But I want you to show up as all that you are, no more and no less.

When you show up as who you are in all your greatness, you will change the atmosphere of every room you walk into. You don't have to dim your light to please anybody else—let your brilliance shine as brightly as you choose, for your own sake. You are deserving of everything that life has to offer, and rest assured, you will attain it all.

# Time to Write It Out

*In this moment, how can you show up big when it seems like everybody wants you to be small?*

........................................................................................

........................................................................................

........................................................................................

........................................................................................

........................................................................................

........................................................................................

........................................................................................

........................................................................................

........................................................................................

........................................................................................

........................................................................................

........................................................................................

........................................................................................

........................................................................................

........................................................................................

........................................................................................

*Pretty Prayer*

**Step out as yourself, as all that you are.**

# DAY SEVENTY-EIGHT

## You Are Creative

I never really understood what creativity meant until I watched Jim Carrey. Even as an adult, I was like a kid in a candy store watching this daring, bold man go for it all. No limits. His mind jumps around just like mine does, like a roller coaster of fun. He inspired me. Before him, I never really understood my gift—all I knew was that I was different. I knew I had something special about me, but I didn't know what I would do with this mind that is always making up stories and doing the most outrageous things. My mind was so creative, but I didn't understand how I could use it. People would tell me, "Girl, you're crazy," and I wondered if maybe they were right.

Whoever is reading this—you're not crazy; you're creative. You've been given something special, but to use it, you have to unlock it with God. Because the world will suffocate your creativity if you let them. The world will shrink you, will tell you there's something wrong with you when there's not. You're not crazy; you're gifted.

If you have something special about you and you're trying to create an opportunity—whatever it might be— just know that you have to protect it. You hold a gift inside you that no one else does. Some people aren't going to get it. Some people won't understand you. And you know what? That's a *good* thing. Because if your gift and your purpose don't scare somebody? Then you're not pushing hard enough. Get out there! It's okay to be weird and different! It's okay to stand out in your own mode! Stand tall, embrace your weirdness, and dare to be different.

## Time to Write It Out
*In this moment, how will you let loose with your creativity?*

........................................................................................

........................................................................................

........................................................................................

........................................................................................

........................................................................................

........................................................................................

........................................................................................

........................................................................................

........................................................................................

........................................................................................

........................................................................................

........................................................................................

*Pretty Prayer*

**Who cares what anyone thinks? Go be gifted.**

# DAY SEVENTY-NINE

## Stand on Your Faith and Your Truth

Baby, your promise is secured.

If you have faith in anything, you can have faith in this: Your promise was given to you by God. It is there waiting for you. Yes, there's a process you have to go through, and it isn't always easy. So if things are tough right now, if it's all feeling like work and struggle—okay, cool, that's a sign you're in your process. It is *not* a sign that you're headed down a dead-end street.

I know you're not doubting God. So who are you doubting when you're sitting around chewing your nails and procrastinating and not actually getting anything done?

The person you're doubting is *you*. You're worrying you don't have what it takes. That your gift isn't good enough. That you're not strong enough or smart enough or committed enough to make your dreams come true.

But why would you get in your own way like that? Why would you let self-doubt, anxiety, and fear rule you? You've got to stand on what you know and have faith.

Here's what I know: You are brave. You are powerful. You are full of beauty, creativity, passion, and intelligence. All of that is within you—that's part of your promise, and it was given to you from the beginning.

All you have to do is keep reaching out. Embrace the faith that you already possess, and trust in the process. It's in these trials and tribulations that you will discover the depths of your own resilience and the limitless potential within you. Stand tall.

## Time to Write It Out
*In this moment, how will you stand on what you know?*

_Pretty Prayer_

**Your promise is secured.**

# Redirect

You think you've got a plan. You've got it all worked out—you're gonna flow from one step to the next, and because you put in the effort, it's all gonna go great for you. Only . . . that's not what happens. God re-directs you, sends you on a different path, and if you don't keep your faith, that can feel like failure. That can feel like you've lost your chance, that you're not gonna make it.

Lord, Lord, Lord, Lord! You've got to build your faith! You've got say, "All right, God. I guess You want me to do something else, huh?"

When God redirected me away from my plan—to do radio, to be the next Wendy Williams or Steve Harvey—I thought that meant I didn't have what it took to be a suc-cess in the entertainment industry. But that was just be-cause my focus was on being behind the camera, not in front of it—and God had a different plan for me. He said, "No, baby, that's not really what you want." He knew how much I was going to *love* being on camera and the way my physical comedy would play a part in my performance! He understood my gift better than I did.

We pray for what we love and desire and need, and God does answer us—but He sees further than we do, deeper than we do, and with more truth than we ever could. He redirects us to bring us higher, to let the whole world see and hear us.

## Time to Write It Out

*In this moment, how will you trust God when He guides you on your path?*

........................................................................................

........................................................................................

........................................................................................

........................................................................................

........................................................................................

........................................................................................

........................................................................................

........................................................................................

........................................................................................

........................................................................................

........................................................................................

........................................................................................

........................................................................................

........................................................................................

*Pretty Prayer*

**Your redirection was a part of your protection.
Trust God. Lord, Lord, Lord!**

# *Victorious Friends*

## *What Makes You Victorious?*

*Two things that can contribute to victory are determination and preparation. Determination keeps you focused on your goals despite obstacles, and preparation ensures you're ready for all the challenges that come your way. This is why I can give Momma whatever she wants. The love I have for my family will always remind me to be victorious.*

SHAQUILLE O'NEAL, retired NBA champion, entrepreneur, and media icon

*My faith in God.*

LIL DUVAL, comedian, actor, and recording artist

*I am victorious because Victory is all I see. Late Victory, slow Victory, even postponed Victory, but nothing else.*

KATT WILLIAMS, Emmy Award–winning stand-up comedian, actor, producer, and entrepreneur

*Victory is defeating the enemy in any form—overcoming obstacles or struggles that are actually meant to challenge us, challenge our faith, challenge our ability to endure.*

JESS HILARIOUS, comedian, actress, content creator, and radio star

*My legacy, my work ethic, my growth, my discipline, my success, and my heart.*

LISARAYE MCCOY, actress, TV personality, fashion designer, humanitarian, entrepreneur, and director

*Any type of win or achievement for those I love . . . Being counted out and left to fail, but I pushed through and reached higher levels than I intended to.*

TRAE THA TRUTH, Billboard Music Award–winning artist, rapper, activist, and philanthropist

*I am victorious because I'm fueled by the love of God. I don't allow setbacks to cloud my view of the finish line. I understand that mistakes have the power to make us into something better than we were before. I am victorious because through it all . . . I rise.*

DR. AMIRA OGUNLEYE, award-winning cosmetic dentist and mentor

# Trust God, Even Though You Don't See Him

*Okay, God, where You at? Do You even hear me? Do You hear my prayers?*

If you feel like you're talking to an empty room, if nothing you're doing feels supported by your faith, or if you've been working for so long and it seems like you're still not moving forward—*be still. Hold on. It's all right.*

Even when you don't see Him, hear Him, or feel Him, I know God is there for you.

When I get to feeling that way, I go looking for Him, and let me tell you, God is not hard to find. I smell my flowers, and I smell God. I go to my refrigerator and eat my fruit, and how good it makes me feel. That's God too. I go for a walk and hear the birds singing and people laughing and talking with each other, watch the leaves moving in the breeze, and breathe in all that fresh air—all of it is faith building.

We don't get to see God face-to-face like we do our friends and family, the people who support us. But here's a Pretty Truth: *People will fail you. Your mama, your daddy, your auntie, and your grandma—they will all fail you, because they are human and imperfect. But the one person we don't see? He will never fail us.*

Build your faith in this season. Build your belief system. Hold on to the strength that it gives you to see you through the hard times, so you can remember that even when you don't see Him, even when you don't understand what He is doing for you, God is working for your good.

## Time to Write It Out
*In this moment, how will you build your faith?*

........................................................................................................
........................................................................................................
........................................................................................................
........................................................................................................
........................................................................................................
........................................................................................................
........................................................................................................
........................................................................................................
........................................................................................................
........................................................................................................
........................................................................................................
........................................................................................................
........................................................................................................
........................................................................................................

*Pretty Prayer*

**This is your faith-building season.**

## DAY EIGHTY-TWO

# Be Inspired and Don't Compete

Somebody else's success doesn't make it any more or less likely that *you'll* be successful—it has nothing at all to do with you. The world is abundant with opportunities for everybody to thrive. There's enough money, joy, creativity, and passion to go around. So just because you see someone out there who is creative doesn't mean *your* ideas are any less imaginative.

I am uniquely made. God made me like *me*. My courage is different from anyone else's. My walk, my creativity, my purpose—they are all mine and nobody else's. No one can be like me—and no one can be like you either. And here's a Pretty Truth: *If you try to be like another person, you will diminish yourself.* Trying to mimic someone's path to success is not the way to achieve genuine fulfillment and accomplishment.

It's easy to imitate somebody's ideas, attitude, and sauce—it's right there for you to model yourself after. But even if you gain followers or recognition by copying them, it won't truly be *your* success, because it won't reflect your unique gifts and essence. It won't be *you*. Instead, have the courage to step out with what *you* have to share. The world will be greater for it—and just watch; your success will be greater too. Success is always more profound and meaningful when it's a reflection of your true self.

## Time to Write It Out

*In this moment, how can you avoid comparing yourself to others?*

........................................................................................

........................................................................................

........................................................................................

........................................................................................

........................................................................................

........................................................................................

........................................................................................

........................................................................................

........................................................................................

........................................................................................

........................................................................................

........................................................................................

........................................................................................

........................................................................................

*Pretty Prayer*

**You're the only one who can be you.**

# DAY EIGHTY-THREE

## You Lead–the Rest Will Follow

Growing up, I felt like no one took me seriously. It made sense—I was all over the place, cracking jokes, playing around. I didn't have a care in the world, and I was always certain my mom was going to take care of everything for me. But as I got closer to my purpose, I watched myself grow, both professionally and spiritually. And I began to notice that when I spoke, my friends would listen. When I led, my friends would follow.

I'm not coming from a place of cockiness or arrogance—I'm not some *Mean Girls* drama queen having people follow me because it makes *me* feel good. They follow because they know that where I'm going, they deserve to be there too. They know that I am leading them to their greatness. I am bringing them from a comfortable space to an uncomfortable one because I wholeheartedly want my people to reach their potential, and they know I can help them get there. If I'm not leading, then I'm just taking up space.

Do you have friends who are going to pull you to the next level, make you uncomfortable, lead you to your victorious season? I know I'm that friend—are you that friend? You have to be a leader, not a follower. You have to be above, not beneath. And once you know that you are victorious inside, your friends and family will follow. Even your haters will follow. You have it in you to lead. You can lead with grace, passion, authenticity, and humility. People will follow you not because they have to but because they believe in you. They believe in the journey that you are all embarking on together.

## Time to Write It Out
*In this moment, how will you lead the people around you?*

.............................................................................................
.............................................................................................
.............................................................................................
.............................................................................................
.............................................................................................
.............................................................................................
.............................................................................................
.............................................................................................
.............................................................................................
.............................................................................................
.............................................................................................
.............................................................................................

*Pretty Prayer*

**You have leadership in you too. Just activate it.**

# DAY EIGHTY-FOUR

## Transform Your Mind

The brain is a beautiful thing, holding our thoughts, emotions, intelligence, and memories, helping us sift through all of that and live our very best lives. But sometimes, it feels like the mind is working against you, like your doubts and insecurities are taking over. When this happens, take a second to really look at those thoughts, not just accept them as true. Is this reality? Or is your head playing tricks on you? Because I can tell you that nine times out of ten, it's just some negative energy pushing you away from what you know God has in store for you.

Maybe things didn't work out quite the way you wanted, so your mind is telling you that you're a failure. *No!* You took one L. That's okay. That doesn't mean you should quit. It doesn't mean you're not capable. Those doubts and insecurities and all those negative thoughts you're having? Baby, you have to give them to God. And then you keep pushing, being thankful for your abilities and grateful for what you've learned so you can be better next time.

Your mind will tell you lies and try to keep you from your destiny. It'll try to hold you back with past traumas and paralyze you from walking into your next season. So you have to choose to put great thoughts in place and use them to shove the negative thoughts away. Speak affirmations over your body, your life, your success. You have the power to shape your reality to match the vision God has given you. You have been called to a higher place, so you must raise your thoughts to match. You *can* persevere if you transform your mind. Your *yes* is around the corner—you just gotta go get it.

## Time to Write It Out
*In this moment, what affirmations can you speak over yourself?*

........................................................................................

........................................................................................

........................................................................................

........................................................................................

........................................................................................

........................................................................................

........................................................................................

........................................................................................

........................................................................................

*Pretty Prayer*

**It is imperative to renew your mind. Don't listen to thoughts of the enemy. You got this!**

# DAY EIGHTY-FIVE

## Don't Believe Those Lies

One thing about my mama—she cannot stand a liar, and she brought me up the same way. Whether it's someone capping about all the things they had or these crazy blog sites with their rumors, I can't stand them. I've never understood why it's so hard for some people to tell the truth.

But what about the lies that exist within us? Like the ones that are telling you you're not good enough or aren't smart enough?

You'd better not believe them. I hope you know they're not true. It doesn't matter who first told you that you couldn't do it. It doesn't matter who said it wasn't possible. The next time you hear those voices again, the next time those lies pop in, I want you to say, "The devil is a liar." I want you to remember that you were created by God to live out your fullest potential. Don't let a lie stop that.

I used to always try to figure out, *Is this a gift, or is my mind just playing tricks on me?* I had to learn to trust God and trust my own truth, not the lies of the enemy. Because here's your Pretty Truth: *You are victorious. You are made unique, with your own purpose and calling.* There will never be a point in your life when God will exist within a lie. God is truth and can only dwell within the truth, because He is not an author of confusion—He's an author of peace. When you're feeling down and you start to believe that every lie stated about you is truth, remember that God is *light*, and He will bring the sunshine to cast out all the darkness in your story.

## Time to Write It Out

*In this moment, how will you find God's truth amid the lies?*

.............................................................................................

.............................................................................................

.............................................................................................

.............................................................................................

.............................................................................................

.............................................................................................

.............................................................................................

.............................................................................................

.............................................................................................

.............................................................................................

.............................................................................................

.............................................................................................

.............................................................................................

*Pretty Prayer*

**God is truth.**

# Standing on Business

I see you. I see the hurt, the insecurities, the fears. I see the pain behind your smile.

That smile is a mask you put on every day to hide your true self—because you worry the real you isn't good enough or is too vulnerable, too scared. You think that mask protects you—but it doesn't. It's only holding you back.

It's time to shake off that mask and stand on business. Don't be afraid to be yourself. Don't be afraid to show the world who you really are, and don't be afraid to be vulnerable in this season. It's okay to show your vulnerabilities! They are a part of your story—a part of what makes you beautifully human. It's time to stand tall, own your truth, and reclaim your power.

If you gotta cry it out—do it! Shout, scream, do what you have to do to release all that sadness, all that anger and trauma. Because if you keep stuffing it back behind that mask of a smile, it's only going to suffocate you. Let it go, and liberate yourself. You are strong, and you will get through this.

Authenticity is a superpower that can change your life. When you allow yourself to be genuine with the people around you, you will be able to create true connection with them, opening space for meaningful relationships where love, compassion, and grace can exist.

Here's my Pretty Truth: *You are standing before a door. On the other side of it is the liberated, released, and authentic you. All you have to do is step out of hiding and walk through it.*

## Time to Write It Out

*In this moment, how will you release your pain?*

................................................................................

................................................................................

................................................................................

................................................................................

................................................................................

................................................................................

................................................................................

................................................................................

................................................................................

................................................................................

................................................................................

................................................................................

................................................................................

*Pretty Prayer*

**Pause and just breathe through it!**

# DAY EIGHTY-SEVEN

## Validate Yourself

We spend so much time and energy searching for validation, constantly seeking reassurance from other people: *Am I good at this? Someone tell me I'm funny. Someone tell me I'm pretty. Someone tell me I'm smart, kind, brave. Someone let me know that they see me for who I am.*

But I gotta ask you: Do *you* see yourself? Do you see how brave you are? Do you see your own kindness and intelligence and beauty? Because here's a Pretty Truth: *If you don't, then it doesn't matter how many people shower you with compliments and affirmations—you won't ever really believe them, not deep down in your heart.* You'll always be searching for more external validation, and nothing anybody else tells you will ever be enough.

To break free from this cycle, you've got to learn to validate yourself. You've got to look inside and see who you really are, in all your glory, and genuinely feel and believe in your own worth. And when doubt tries to creep in, you have to be able to search inside yourself and say, *I have this. I am this. I will overcome this.* Once you can do that, everything else will fall into place.

Whenever you feel empty, you will have the ability to fill yourself up. You won't have to rely on external sources for your sense of self-worth and fulfillment. You'll be self-sufficient and self-assured, knowing that you are more than enough, just as you are.

## Time to Write It Out
*In this moment, how can you validate yourself?*

................................................................................
................................................................................
................................................................................
................................................................................
................................................................................
................................................................................
................................................................................
................................................................................
................................................................................
................................................................................
................................................................................
................................................................................
................................................................................

*Pretty Prayer*

**You can tell yourself what you need to hear.**

# DAY EIGHTY-EIGHT

# The Time Has Changed but the Pain Hasn't

You know how they say "Time heals all wounds"? That's wrong. I'm calling BS on that. Time is not enough to make your pain go away.

I know you know that already, because you're still thinking about your pain. You're thinking, *I should forgive them; I should forgive myself,* but you can't, because you still have pain way down deep inside you. The pain from being bullied in the third grade, from being molested, from facing rejection from your mom and dad—it was all a long time ago, but all that fear and trauma is still in you.

You're not going to heal from it unless you give it to God. Releasing that pain is how you know that you're worthy. It's how you're going to keep getting up in the morning.

I get it. I know it's easier said than done, because I've been through it too. But I overcame what happened to me, so I understand where you are. What I don't understand is why you can't give yourself grace. Why you don't know that God has given you the strength to move into better days ahead. Time is constantly moving, and you gotta move with it. You don't want to stay stuck with that pain. Your pain doesn't have an address in you. But you have to *believe* that and give your pain to God. He can take it, and in exchange He'll give you back yourself, free in all your beauty.

## Time to Write It Out
*In this moment, how can you give your pain to God?*

........................................................................

........................................................................

........................................................................

........................................................................

........................................................................

........................................................................

........................................................................

........................................................................

........................................................................

........................................................................

........................................................................

........................................................................

........................................................................

........................................................................

*Pretty Prayer*

**Trouble don't last always! –Rev. Timothy Wright**

# DAY EIGHTY-NINE

## Fear Is *Not* Your Portion

Don't you love Thanksgiving? You got your mac and cheese, your collard greens and candied yams, your turkey and your stuffing. But you know what had better not be on your plate? It'd better not be fear! Fear can stagnate you. It holds you back with all that second-guessing. Fear will not allow your dreams to come true.

Fear is not your portion in this season. God has not designed you to hold fear. That's why it hurts you to carry it, why it holds you back from your greatness—it was never meant for you. Those fearful thoughts are the enemy speaking to you, and you need to tune out that noise.

I know what fear looks like. There have been times when I almost allowed my thoughts to stop me, but I always got to the other end and realized what was meant for me. I was not meant to consume and be consumed by fear. I was meant for greatness, for victory—and I know you are too.

You know your auntie who can't cook? The one whose food you secretly throw in the trash can? That's exactly what I want you to do with that plate of fear. Fear is an unwelcome course in the feast of your life, and it has no place on your table. You go fill yourself up with only good things, things that will nourish your body and soul—like confidence, faith, determination, and positivity. Fill yourself up with greatness, and step into your victory.

## Time to Write It Out
*In this moment, how can you cast away your fears?*

_____

_____

_____

_____

_____

_____

_____

_____

_____

_____

_____

_____

_____

*Pretty Prayer*

**There's a whole lot of fear but not enough faith on your plate. What will be your portion this season?**

# DAY NINETY

## Unleash Your Own Potential

Everybody has their own hidden gift, but some people are afraid to show it. Maybe they're afraid their gift won't make money, or they've been told that's not a real job.

Not you. It's time for you to unleash your potential. It's time to let the whole world see you as you step into the spotlight and let yourself shine. No more being scared and fearful. No more worrying about the what-ifs. No more thinking you're going to be denied or rejected. It's time to brighten, to be beautiful, to be a butterfly. It's time to fly, baby!

You've been rejecting yourself before anybody else even got the chance! You haven't even been out there so everybody can see you—so how do you know what they're going to say? Sure, not everybody will get you—who cares? The ones who matter, they will *love you*. God gave you this gift to share with the world, not to hide away like it's yours alone. Hiding your light is selfish—you are denying the glory that is *you,* and the people around you deserve to experience you in all your greatness.

You've been holding yourself back, but it's time to cast aside all that's been stopping you. Don't second-guess what you know is for you. It's time to get on with your life! There's an opportunity with your name on it, but you're the one who needs to get off that bed, stop watching *Moesha* reruns all day, and go get it!

## Time to Write It Out
*In this moment, how will you stop hiding and shine your light?*

........................................................................................

........................................................................................

........................................................................................

........................................................................................

........................................................................................

........................................................................................

........................................................................................

........................................................................................

........................................................................................

........................................................................................

........................................................................................

*Pretty Prayer*

**Your potential is within you. Let it out!**

# DAY NINETY-ONE

# Stand on What You Know

Once I got my first big break, I was so happy and excited to finally be *in*. I thought, *I made it! I'm gonna be known; I'm gonna be the girl in the room that everybody wants to talk to. I'll be a magnet, bringing everyone to me, making them all laugh.* And that turned out to be true—but it wasn't the whole story. Because yeah, people wanted to talk to me inside that room, but outside that room? Nobody cared.

I learned the hard truth of the entertainment industry: When somebody's eating, they won't feed you. They won't baby you if you don't understand. They won't sit beside you when you're alone. I had to do all of that for myself, because it sure wasn't gonna come from them. If you're creating content on social media and trying to put yourself out there and get noticed, the same thing can happen to you—you might feel surrounded by love one moment and lost and alone the next.

So I've got to ask you: Do you have what it takes? I'm not asking whether you have the gift, because I know you do. I mean, do you have the inner strength to stay true to yourself when everybody's trying to push you to change? I thank God that my feet are on the ground, that I came into this industry as myself, and that I will leave the same way. People came at me, wanting me to change, to make choices that would have sacrificed my values and my integrity and chipped away at my beliefs—but I stood firm and stayed true to who I am.

You've got to do the same. You've got to put yourself out there to make it big—but you've got to stay yourself. You've got to stand on what you know and hold true to your authenticity.

## Time to Write It Out
*In this moment, what does being true to yourself look like?*

.................................................................................

.................................................................................

.................................................................................

.................................................................................

.................................................................................

.................................................................................

.................................................................................

.................................................................................

.................................................................................

.................................................................................

*Pretty Prayer*

**Come as yourself and leave as yourself.**

# Do Things You've Never Done Before

When I first started getting paychecks, all I did was work. I thought that was what I needed to do to succeed—this was my shot, and I wasn't going to waste it. *Work, work, work, work, work.* That's all I did. It was a whirlwind of hustle and ambition, and I was determined not to let a single moment slip by without giving it my all.

But then I started seeing friends and people I looked up to—people who worked just as hard as I did or even harder—who were burning out. They were exhausted, and their work just wasn't as good because there was no life to it anymore.

I didn't want that to happen to me. I didn't want to sacrifice my well-being and happiness on the altar of ambition. So in 2022, I told myself I was going to take some time to just be present. I was going to have fun, to live with what God gave me. I was going to walk in new air and learn different cultures. Instead of constantly chasing the next milestone, I made a commitment to myself to enjoy the journey, to bask in the richness of life itself.

When you're working so hard all the time, it becomes easy to forget that you actually have the ability to live. You can still go out and do things—in fact, you're supposed to! Life is meant to be lived, not just survived. It's about more than ticking off items on a to-do list. It's about finding balance, cultivating meaningful connections, and nourishing your soul with experiences that bring you joy. So don't get so caught up in always putting one foot in front of the other. Take a step sideways once in a while. Do it for you.

## Time to Write It Out

*In this moment, how will you live your life instead of surviving it?*

........................................................................................

........................................................................................

........................................................................................

........................................................................................

........................................................................................

........................................................................................

........................................................................................

........................................................................................

........................................................................................

*Pretty Prayer*

**Step out to step forward.**

# A Big Part of Elevation Is Association

Who are you rolling with? What company are you keeping?

I've been hustling for over a decade now, and I've been surrounded by so many pioneers, legends, and superstars—and when I stand beside them, it's not just because I want a good picture to post on social media. It's because as I stand there, I become one of them. These are relationships that elevate me, that inspire and drive me toward growing and improving.

There is power in the folks that you stand with, and sometimes that means stepping out of one circle to go stand in another. I had to change my circle when I changed seasons, because I needed the uplift of something unfamiliar, something that made me uncomfortable. Leaving old things behind often makes room for newer, greater energy to come into your life. These pioneers are now people I consider family and friends, though I am always a student first. Let me ask you, would you rather have $500,000 or a chance to have dinner with Jay-Z? I would *absolutely* go eat with Jay-Z so I can access his knowledge and wisdom. You cannot buy that for any price.

Choosing to spend your time with people who elevate

you isn't "acting Hollywood" or betraying where you came from—it's just that you want more for yourself in this season, and that's okay. It's okay to leave things behind. Keep friends that will move with you as you grow. Maybe your old friends still do that for you, and that's great! But ask yourself, *Who am I associating with that's gonna elevate me? Who will inspire me?* And if you're not getting that from your friends, then leave them right where they are.

## Time to Write It Out
*In this moment, how will you surround yourself with people who inspire and elevate you?*

........................................................................................................

........................................................................................................

........................................................................................................

........................................................................................................

........................................................................................................

........................................................................................................

........................................................................................................

........................................................................................................

*Pretty Prayer*

**Are your friends elevating you in this season? If not, change circles.**

# DAY NINETY-FOUR

---

# Don't Read the Room;
# Lead the Room

I want you to walk into every room like God sent you there.

Has anybody ever told you that you need to build your confidence? Has somebody lowered your self-esteem? Did anyone break you down to the core to make you feel small?

It's time to take your confidence back. Stop playing in the back when God wants you to be in front. Stop playing second when God wants you first. Stop leaning on plan B when God wants you to finish plan A.

And most importantly, stop looking at what everybody else is doing to figure out what you should do—just do it. Walk into that room and own it.

Every room I walk into, my head is held high. My mother taught me that, and it wasn't from the pageants I participated in or the school uniforms I wore at Lawton Chiles Middle School, or that new pair of Jordans I put on my feet. My head was high because every day my inner voice was telling me I was beautiful. Holding God in me made me feel like I could go into any room with my back straight.

By walking into a room with your head high and your back straight, you are calling in authority. You're saying,

"Oh, baby, move out of my way, please." That room is yours already—all you gotta do is own it. Stop trying to play in the back. Stop listening to the lies and the enemy in your mind. Claim what's yours, write the check, sign the deal, and walk into every room like you're the boss.

## Time to Write It Out

*In this moment, how will you hold your head high?*

..........................................................................................................
..........................................................................................................
..........................................................................................................
..........................................................................................................
..........................................................................................................
..........................................................................................................
..........................................................................................................
..........................................................................................................
..........................................................................................................
..........................................................................................................
..........................................................................................................
..........................................................................................................
..........................................................................................................

*Pretty Prayer*

**You're a giant in spirit. Own it.**

# Everybody Wants a Piece of Your Attention

Everybody will want a piece of your blessing. That attention you're getting? They're gonna want some of that. What God has blessed you with? They're gonna think it's theirs too. God gave you determination, faith, drive—and I want you to ask yourself why you should have to share all that. God didn't give those gifts to them; He gave them to *you*.

I had twenty friends when I got out of college, and I can name only two of them now. The rest? They were secretly jealous, secretly hating on me. They were the kind of friends your mother and grandmother warn you about, who want to take from you. The ones who listen to your ideas but then, the next day, go out and do all that you said *you* were gonna do, before you even got the chance. You planted seeds in these friends' minds, and now they're sprouting and you're being left behind.

I had to say to those friends, "You are not deserving of my blessings, of what God gave to me. Why are you trying to take that away? Why are you seeking to take the attention that I worked for and earned? How dare you get jealous of what God is doing for me! How dare you act differently around me when I'm getting blessed. Wait your turn!"

God gave you a gift, and that means you have to protect it. You need to have the space to cultivate your gift without worrying that someone's going to try to take it away from you. The gift that is in you doesn't belong to anyone but you. Tell your friends to go find their own. Period.

## Time to Write It Out
*In this moment, how will you protect your blessings?*

--------------------------------------------------------

--------------------------------------------------------

--------------------------------------------------------

--------------------------------------------------------

--------------------------------------------------------

--------------------------------------------------------

--------------------------------------------------------

--------------------------------------------------------

--------------------------------------------------------

--------------------------------------------------------

--------------------------------------------------------

--------------------------------------------------------

*Pretty Prayer*

**Ask God to bring you a circle of bosses.**

# DAY NINETY-SIX

# In the Midst of Your Shift, Be Still

I hate the word *still*. When I got in trouble as a kid, I hated being put in time-out. "Be still. Don't move. Wait for a second. I'll be right with you; can you hold on?" I hated all of those words as a kid, and to be honest, I still do. I want to *move*, to do it all—but I force myself to take a seat, because I know that God will speak to me when I'm still.

We move so much and don't stop to think about where we are, to hear what God is saying to us. Sometimes all that moving around is a form of distraction, and what we're moving toward isn't even in the right direction—but we don't know that because we're not taking the time to sit still so we can hear God.

God's knocking on your door, asking, "Can I just get minutes of your time?" Meanwhile, you're moving on your own time. There's a shift happening in your life right now, and you're questioning it because you don't know where it's coming from. Baby, that shift is from God. You won't have any more setbacks, but you have to wait a second and hear from God so you know which way to move. Stop running all around with everybody else, not listening, like me when I was a kid. Those same people are gonna be at the club! But you—you gotta focus.

Will you be still so you can hear God's voice?

# Time to Write It Out

*In this moment, how will you be still so you know how to move?*

...................................................................................

...................................................................................

...................................................................................

...................................................................................

...................................................................................

...................................................................................

...................................................................................

...................................................................................

...................................................................................

...................................................................................

...................................................................................

...................................................................................

...................................................................................

...................................................................................

...................................................................................

...................................................................................

...................................................................................

*Pretty Prayer*

**Today, are you gonna give God
five minutes of your time?**

## DAY NINETY-SEVEN

# God Is About to Enlarge
# Your Territory

At church, I used to always hear my mom say, "God's gonna enlarge your territory. He's gonna give you everything your heart desires. He's not gonna let you go without. He will expand you." I heard it all—and she was right.

God is going to take you beyond your seat, but you have to believe that He will. Because you might not see it even while it's happening. Getting fired from a job? How's God gonna enlarge that? When things like that happen (as they do to everybody), you might feel like you don't have hope or trust. How can you trust the words of people who keep failing you? And that's true—you can't. But you *can* trust God.

You are granted this favor. You are already walking toward your destiny. Something that feels like a setback, like you're heading backward, is actually something for God to expand on. He's taking you where you need to go. Maybe you've been working on an idea for ten years and you're not seeing anything coming out of it—but that doesn't mean God isn't working for you. He's just trying to see what your faith looks like. He's trying to see if you're going to be obedient in your season, if you can let go of old habits and old people. He's gotta see whether you're ready for it before He gives it to you in full.

I don't have all the answers. I don't know *how* you're going to get where you're going—but I do know that there is a God who will help you, teach you, expand you, and enlarge your territory. He's doing it right now.

## Time to Write It Out
*In this moment, how will you trust God and show your faith?*

........................................................................................................

........................................................................................................

........................................................................................................

........................................................................................................

........................................................................................................

........................................................................................................

........................................................................................................

........................................................................................................

........................................................................................................

........................................................................................................

........................................................................................................

........................................................................................................

*Pretty Prayer*

**You have limitless blessings. When God gives them to you, you'd better take care of them.**

# DAY NINETY-EIGHT

## It's Go Time

Ready, set, go!

Close this damn book, get in the shower, get in the car, and go chase that opportunity. It's go time.

But wait—real quick, before you close it . . .

Remember, ain't no more procrastinating, second-guessing, calling your friends or your mama, saying, "What do you think . . . ?" No more.

You can't control what God has for you. You've been dreaming on your success—and that means you've been sleeping on it. God has given you so many resources, and you haven't been using them. That's done now.

You've been reading this book and getting motivated, and now it's time to put actions behind all those thoughts.

It's signed off, got my signature, stamped—it's Pretty Vee. And it's *go time*.

# Time to Write It Out

*In this moment, what's your game plan once you get out the door and go?*

........................................................................................................
........................................................................................................
........................................................................................................
........................................................................................................
........................................................................................................
........................................................................................................
........................................................................................................
........................................................................................................
........................................................................................................
........................................................................................................
........................................................................................................
........................................................................................................
........................................................................................................
........................................................................................................
........................................................................................................
........................................................................................................
........................................................................................................

*Pretty Prayer*

**It's up to you to make your dreams come true.**

# DAY NINETY-NINE

## Turn Your Pain into Victory

I know that you've experienced moments of pain. Maybe it happened publicly, in front of hundreds of people, or privately, when you were left alone. No matter the circumstances, it hurt. All that stuff you went through is a part of you—but it is not *you*.

You have the power to say how it will affect your life. Maybe you haven't realized it yet, but you are already walking in victory. You survived that painful moment, that month, that year, and that season. The enemy thought it would break you, but it only made you a conqueror.

I have shared with you the times I felt like it was all over for me, when I locked so much hurt inside my heart that I was stuck there. I told you about those painful parts of my life so you could see that I am a living testimony. I am living in an answered prayer.

I used to think those long nights of suffering—the tears and rejections and constant noes—were a burden I had to carry with me. But I came to realize that they were blessings. Think about what Jesus had to endure to receive the ultimate glory. Well, we aren't excluded from that! God did not make an exception for His Son or for me, and He's not going to make one for you —but that's because He knows you can make it through. God used my mess and turned it into a message. He used my struggle and turned it into strength, and He used my test and turned it into testimony to inspire all those who experience pain.

You are in your victory season. You are making all the right moves and turning what was once your pain into your strength. Claim your Pretty Victory.

## Time to Write It Out
*In this moment, how can you turn your struggle into strength?*

.................................................................................................
.................................................................................................
.................................................................................................
.................................................................................................
.................................................................................................
.................................................................................................
.................................................................................................
.................................................................................................

*Pretty Prayer*

**God, I pray that the souls reading this book feel important and loved. I pray that they will become who they are destined to be—that right now, they will go be victorious.**

## DAY ONE HUNDRED

# Accept Your Pretty Victory

Congratulations, my victorious friends! You have made it to the end!

You are *victorious.*

You're done being defeated. You know now that you can cross any bridge that comes before you. You can leap over it.

Any setback you encounter is just a setup for a comeback. A delay is not a denial, friend, and you know that in your heart. There is so much that is yet to be written.

Accept your Pretty Victory today. It's here now. It's being offered to you on a platter. Accept your freedom. Accept your empowerment, your ability to overcome any obstacle. You are free, baby girl. You are victorious, baby boy. You made it through these hundred days a warrior. Accept that now is the time to launch the brand-new you, to walk in your purpose where you know that the enemy cannot hold you back. You are whole. You are destined. You are worthy. You are great. You have everything you need. It is so, and it is done.

You are victorious. You are chosen.

# Time to Write It Out

*In this moment, how will you accept that you are victorious and free?*

........................................................................................

........................................................................................

........................................................................................

........................................................................................

........................................................................................

........................................................................................

........................................................................................

........................................................................................

........................................................................................

........................................................................................

........................................................................................

........................................................................................

........................................................................................

........................................................................................

........................................................................................

*Pretty Prayer*

**You are victorious! But if ever you don't feel that way, it's okay–just pick up this book and start again.**

# Victorious Friends

## What Makes You Victorious?

*I wake up. I already win when I wake up because so many people don't get to wake up. I thank God I get a chance to be better and better every day.*

> TIFFANY HADDISH, Grammy- and Emmy Award–winning comedian, actress, and author

*My belief is stronger than your doubt.*

> DWYANE WADE, former basketball star and three-time NBA champion

*Helping people who're not entitled. Great rest. Beautiful locations. Informative information. Having people in my life I can trust without any doubt!*

> WALLO267, motivational speaker, author, social media personality, business owner, and podcast host

*I feel most victorious when I am living my truth. Following my gut. Trusting my instincts.*

> JACOB LATIMORE, actor and singer

*I win. I may fail along the way. But I always win.*

DETAVIO SAMUELS, CEO of Revolt

*Whenever I sit on a chair, I never shake it or look at the bottom to ensure the screws are tight. I just sit in it. That's because I have faith that it will hold me. I refuse to have more faith in a chair than in myself, especially knowing what my God can do. I'm victorious because I spoke it a long time ago, and I don't give myself enough room to debate it or create fear around it. Once I align with God and speak it into the world, it's done. Victory is mine.*

TASHA HILTON, senior director of brand marketing
and strategy at BET and VH1

*What makes me victorious is my struggle. Knowing what I have been through—I overcame the worst and I'm still overcoming—lets me know that I'm God's child. I know that even my hardest struggles will eventually turn into a victory.*

BOOSIE BADAZZ, rapper, songwriter, and actor

*Love.*

SERAYAH MCNEILL, actress, singer, and model

*Being resilient makes me victorious. It stems from not quitting. From knowing that I serve a God who lets me know that I can do all things, through Christ who strengthens me. This is a part of my victorious walk, and I will forever trust God on this journey.*

PASTOR G, my mommy

# Pretty Challenge

## Write to Yourself

### Why I Won't Give Up

_____

_____

_____

_____

_____

_____

_____

_____

_____

_____

_____

_____

_____

_____

_____

_____

_____

_____

# CONCLUSION

You know, I was so nervous to write this book. These messages come from deep inside me, from my childhood and my life and my faith, from the time I was a kid to now. To be honest, I was scared to let people in close to see all that! But I knew I couldn't let fear stand in my way—I couldn't let it stop me from helping so many souls around the world. I've overcome so many fears in my life, got myself up out of the deep hole of depression, and lived my life with purpose, using my gifts: I make people laugh, I inspire them, and I make them stronger than they ever thought they could be.

My comedy helps people, and I believe that with my whole heart. And let me tell you, everybody has a playful heart. Everybody has a childlike sense of humor, even if maybe they haven't tapped into it for a while. Maybe they haven't explored and accepted it. But my final piece of advice to you?

Laugh.

I don't care if your doctor says you've got thyroid issues or whatever . . . If you bust out with one good laugh, that pain through your heart will find relief. That worry in your mind will ease just because you had something good happen. Food is nourishing for the body, but laughter heals the soul.

So you take your laughter medicine every day. You don't have to be a comedian to laugh—you just have to dive into *you*. Surround yourself with friends and family who encourage you, who bring out your inner child and your silliness. All children laugh, and sometimes each of us has to heal our inner child and bring them out to play. Don't let the stress of the world turn you away from your playful heart. Laughter is in everyone. It is in you.

Make no mistake—*hard times will come.*

As I first began to find success, my pastor told me that the prayers that had gotten me this far weren't going to be enough in my next season. He warned me there would be more attacks from the enemy that I would have to overcome—and he was right. Just because I was beginning to be successful didn't mean my doubts or fears went away. It didn't mean things didn't go wrong sometimes.

Things are going to go wrong for you too. As you climb higher, you have to build up your faith to support you. It will be the scaffold you can rest on when you start to have doubts and forget that your delays are not denials or when you're so lost in the process that you forget about your promise.

I wrote this book for those times. Now that you've finished these hundred days, you have all that knowledge inside you, all that power and inspiration. And these devotionals are here waiting for you whenever you need them. They are something you can always come back to, truths to encourage you on your journey. Everything I've written here—about doubt, friendship, love, adversity, fear, strength, and faith?

I have *lived* all of that.

I have *overcome and embraced* all of that.

I am *still learning* all of that.

It's an ongoing process, one that will never be completed. You and me? We will never stop learning. We will never stop growing and improving, getting stronger and more powerful. When the setbacks come, we know we have what it takes to make comebacks.

And don't forget—your community has your back! Surround yourself with people who uplift and inspire you, who believe in your potential and support your successes. Tell your friends about your Pretty Victory—and make sure they buy the book! Tell them about what you carry within you. Inspire them as you embrace each challenge as an opportunity to grow stronger and wiser, knowing that you have the resilience and determination to overcome any obstacle that stands in your way. Look back on the lessons you've learned, and take pride in the progress you've made. Draw strength from your past victories and use them as fuel to propel you forward toward your dreams.

Feel your cup overflowing. Step into your own power and presence—you are the only one who can.

You are the one *to claim you.*

*To save you.*

*To love you.*

*To claim your Pretty Victory.*

# ACKNOWLEDGMENTS

I just want to take the time to acknowledge my mother in all of her strength and ability. If it wasn't for her I would never have written this book. She helped me in so many ways—all of my depression and anxiety? My mother pulled me out of that dark place and helped me find me again. I've watched my mom pray day in and day out, and I watched her speak life over me, and she inspires me every day to be the person she believed I could be.

Family means everything to me, so I want to acknowledge my dad, my brothers, and my sister—thank you for encouraging me, loving on me, and praying over me. You guys have always been my biggest supporters from the very beginning. I hope I made you proud with this one. (I did it!)

To all my prayer warriors, thank you for covering me, thank you for praying for me, thank you for your strength and courage, for fasting with me and also fighting battles with me, and thank you for being a beautiful vessel in this time of my life. I love you guys.

And to my team who dedicated their time and energy, up all hours encouraging me—even when I was so busy, overscheduled and overwhelmed—their readiness to jump in and contribute has been invaluable, and it's truly made a difference in our progress and success.

And to all my friends that said, "Vee, you need to write a book! You need to help souls—they need to hear from you!" Thank you for being my angels of confirmation, and I hope I made you all proud.

To Matthew Benjamin and the whole team at Penguin Random House: Thank you for taking a chance on me, believing in me, and seeing and hearing my vision. I appreciate you and love you.

This book is dedicated to everyone who thought they had lost themselves, who thought they didn't have a voice, anyone who is battling with their own mind—you can get up again. You can be victorious. You find your true path.

And to God, thank you for using me in a mighty way, and thank you for giving me the gift of laughter, the gift of creativity, the gift to motivate and encourage—and now I'm an author! Thank you!

## ABOUT THE AUTHOR

VENA "PRETTY VEE" EXCELL is a multitalented comedian, actress, and philanthropist. She has been a regular cast member on Nick Cannon's *Wild 'N Out* for nine seasons, showcasing her versatility and comedic prowess. She grew up in Miami, Florida, and graduated from the HBCU Saint Augustine's University. She holds an honorary doctorate in humanitarianism from the Global International Alliance. She currently splits her time between Los Angeles, California, and Atlanta, Georgia.

Pretty Vee has been spreading her wings to encourage the world. She is on a mission to pump up our youth to know and understand their worth and to go after everything they want! Pretty Prayers + Pretty Truths = Pretty Victory! Period!

## ABOUT THE TYPE

This book was set in Baskerville, a typeface designed by John Baskerville (1706–75), an amateur printer and typefounder, and cut for him by John Handy in 1750. The type became popular again when the Lanston Monotype Corporation of London revived the classic roman face in 1923. The Mergenthaler Linotype Company in England and the United States cut a version of Baskerville in 1931, making it one of the most widely used typefaces today.